BIKEPACKING SCOTLAND

BIKEPACKING SCOTLAND

20 MULTI-DAY CYCLING ADVENTURES OFF THE BEATEN TRACK

Markus Stitz

VP First published in 2023 by Vertebrate Publishing.

Omega Court, 352 Cemetery Road, Sheffield S11 8FT, United Kingdom.
www.adventurebooks.com

A CIP catalogue record for this book is available from the British Library.

ISBN 978-1-83981-193-7 (Paperback)
ISBN 978-1-83981-194-4 (Ebook)

Front cover: *Josh Ibbett and Philippa Battye on the Isle of Jura* (route 13).

Back cover (L–R): *Looking at the Spittal of Glenshee from the highest point of the Cateran Trail* (route 17);
Invercauld Bridge over the River Dee (route 17); *Capital Trail* (route 05); *view towards the Forth Bridge
at Carlingnose Point Nature Reserve* (route 06); *at Craighouse Pier, Isle of Jura* (route 13).

Previous page: *Josh Ibbett and Philippa Battye going off route on the Isle of Jura.*

Photography by Markus Stitz unless otherwise credited.

Illustration (page xvi) by Emma Kingston.

Route maps created by Lovell Johns Ltd. Contains OS data © Crown copyright and database right 2023.
www.lovelljohns.com

Additional mapping by Active Maps.
www.activemaps.co.uk

Design and production by Jane Beagley, Vertebrate Publishing.

Printed and bound in Europe by Latitude Press.

Vertebrate Publishing is committed to printing on paper from sustainable sources.

FSC
MIX
Paper from
responsible sources
FSC® C014138
www.fsc.org

BIKEPACKING SCOTLAND

20 MULTI-DAY CYCLING ADVENTURES OFF THE BEATEN TRACK

Markus Stitz

VP

Vertebrate Publishing, Sheffield
www.adventurebooks.com

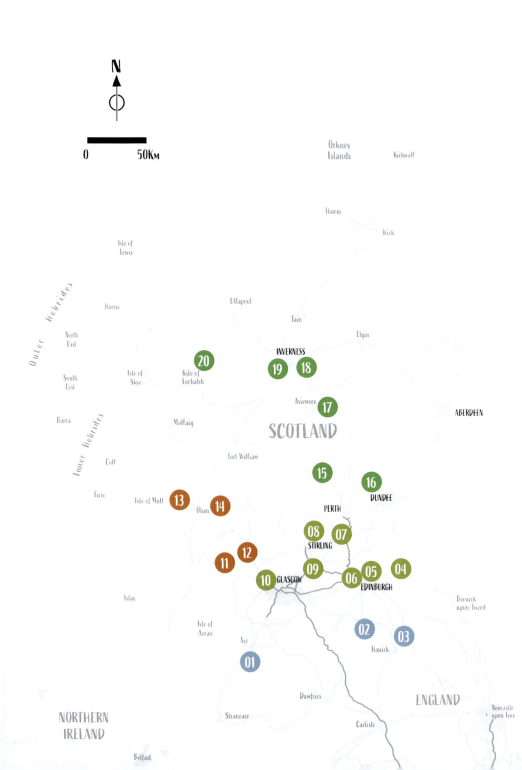

CONTENTS

DOWNLOAD THE BIKEPACKING SCOTLAND
GPX FILES FROM
www.adventurebooks.com/BPS-GPX

ROUTE GRADES (SEE PAGE VIII)

EASY	MEDIUM	HARD
▲	▲	▲

L–R: *Stag on the North Coast 500* (route 20); *mural in Cowdenbeath* (route 06); *Highland cattle in Glen Lonan* (route 12); *camping at Cnuic Charrach on the Isle of Jura* (route 13).

INTRODUCTION

While this is my second book, *Bikepacking Scotland* has been much longer in the making than *Great British Gravel Rides*. I found my love for gravel riding through bikepacking, and in the year before Scotland welcomes the world to the 2023 UCI Cycling World Championships, it seemed fitting to finally write this book.

I had my official introduction to bikepacking in 2014, when I first lined up in Tyndrum to ride the Highland Trail 550 on a single-speed bike. Back then I was unprepared for what lay ahead of me, but I loved the spirit of the community of riders that enveloped me. I had a fair bit of learning to do, but the sheer beauty that surrounded me, and the warm and welcoming nature of both the bikepacking community and the people of Scotland made the experience one that has stuck in my memories ever since.

Shortly after finishing the Highland Trail just hours within the cut-off time, I discovered the Cross Borders Drove Road on one of my local rides in the Pentland Hills. It immediately sparked an interest for the amazing heritage paths that criss-cross the country, and it inspired the development of my first bikepacking route – the Capital Trail.

Only a few months after organising an event on the route in 2015, I was off on a much bigger loop around the world. My 'Extended Capital Trail' took me cycling through 26 different countries and I was met with the same warm hospitality I encountered on my first bikepacking event. But I was also happy and pleased to return to Scotland after 34,000 kilometres (21,126 miles), to combine my passion for bikepacking and my learnings from the trip. This was the start of Bikepacking Scotland.

Since December 2016, when I first registered the domain *bikepackingscotland.com*, I have had the privilege to work with inspiring people across the country to develop and promote bikepacking routes. I came to understand Scotland, which I have called home since 2009, so much better on two wheels than I would have done in any other way.

Bikepacking has allowed me to experience the rich history and natural heritage of the country with all my senses. My work has connected me with inspiring people, many of whom have since become friends. Bikepacking has taken me to the corners of Scotland that the country is world-famous for, but without the need to travel with a metal cage around me. But, more often, cycling has taken me to those places that don't normally feature in other travel guides.

For me, bikepacking is one of the purest ways to discover Scotland off the beaten track, leaving no other trace than a few tyre marks. All the bikepacking adventures I have had in Scotland have created lasting memories, even though at times it was a steep learning experience. Scotland isn't an easy country to cycle in when it throws its weather at you. You will fondly remember the first time you sink your feet into its famous bog, or the first time a cloud of midges surrounds you. But you will also be blown away by the wonderful scenery, no matter where you go.

The routes in this book are only a snapshot. Scotland inspires a vibrant community of people who create routes, organise events or simply share their experiences on social media, and these are people that are proud of where they call home. Its access rights, historic routes and climate make it one of the best countries in the world to enjoy bikepacking.

I hope this book serves as inspiration for you to enjoy your cycling adventures, big and small.

Markus Stitz
Edinburgh, December 2022

FEEDBACK AND UPDATES

If you have any feedback, please do contact me: *markus@bikepackingscotland.com @reizkultur*

ACKNOWLEDGEMENTS

This book wouldn't have been possible without the great input from all the people who have dedicated their time and in-depth knowledge to make *bikepackingscotland.com* happen over the years and for which I am really grateful. I would also like to thank everyone I have forgotten to mention: Clive Drummond, Bill McKinlay, Teyl de Bordes, Elaine Carmichael, Josh Ibbett, Rich Rothwell, Ashley Menzies, Neil Ramsay, Francisco Perez, Gavin Morton, Helen Dick, Andrew Macnair, Cathy Craig, Clare Cooper, Mark Tate, Lindsay Mackinnon, Jason Clark, Sarah Caird, Karen MacCorquodale, Nicky Hesketh, Mike Dennison, Craig Mills, Charlie Hobbs, Maximilian Wussler, Jenny Graham, Mark and Nicci Beaumont, Rory Hitchens, Walter Hamilton, Tim Ward, Kelly-Jayne Collinge, Maciek Tomiczek, Trevor Ward, Christian Urbanski, Christian Simon, Elmar Jünemann, Sebastian Eckardt, Paddy Cuthbert, Graham Sheach, Philippa Battye, Ross O'Reilly, Alan Goldsmith, Mike Stead, Richard Watts, Sally Devlin, Rick Musgrave-Wood, Tori Fahey, Miles Resso, Matt DeNeef, Christian Baumann, Fynn Elkington, Esther Tacke, Warren Saunders, Dougie Hay, Dave Blair, George Lupton, David Hope-Jones, John Pagan and Sabine Guendel.

A special thanks to Ian Ezzi, who inspired many of my early adventures; Louise Chavarie, my partner, best travel buddy and creative director; Carron Tobin, who turned many ideas into reality with funding and sound advice; Jay Lamb, who inspired me making *Bikepacking Scotland* become reality; my family; and Kirsty Reade, John Coefield and everyone at Vertebrate Publishing. Thanks to my sponsors, especially Apidura, Kinesis Bikes UK, komoot, Schwalbe Tyres UK and Exposure Lights.

HOW TO USE THIS BOOK

This book provides descriptions of 20 routes suitable for road, gravel and mountain bikes in Scotland. The rides are presented in roughly geographical order, starting in the south and finishing in the far north. Each route description gives you the following information:

- A short summary of the route.
- A detailed route description, which includes points of interest and historical information.
- Other routes nearby to inspire your own exploration.
- Essential information that includes grade, distance, ascent, start/finish locations with Ordnance Survey grid references and satnav, nearest bike-friendly public transport and the distance from the start/finish, the highest point, terrain information, a percentage comparison of surfaces encountered, recommended bike choice, best time to ride and warnings, where needed.
- Places to stay and eat, as well as bike shops and bike hire options.

Each route portrait is accompanied by beautiful photography to give you a sense of what to expect on your adventure, and, where possible, a QR code to a YouTube video about the route.

ROUTE GRADES

EASY ▲

These routes are a great introduction to bikepacking, suitable for most fitness and skills levels.

MEDIUM ▲

These routes are suitable for riders with good fitness and riding skills.

HARD ▲

These routes are suitable for riders with very good fitness and expert riding skills.

SCOTLAND: A BIKEPACKER'S DREAM

There are many reasons for choosing Scotland as a bikepacking destination: the favourable access rights, the weather, a vast network of historic routes and other great trails, the stunning scenery, the unique bothy network, a rich food and drink culture, and dark skies. But the biggest reason to go bikepacking in Scotland is the warm welcome you will receive wherever you go. Whether you are exploring the streets of Edinburgh or Glasgow, or you end up in a remote Highland village, you are guaranteed a hearty greeting from the locals.

HISTORICAL ROUTES: THE HERITAGE PATHS PROJECT

Scotland has a unique network of heritage paths from bygone times. The Heritage Paths Project from the Scottish Rights of Way and Access Society, ScotWays, started in 2007. ScotWays is the independent charity which upholds and promotes public access rights in Scotland. Its interactive Heritage Path Map (*www.scotways.com/heritage-paths*) is one of the best resources for planning bikepacking adventures in Scotland. The map gives you not only basic information about the state of the paths, but also the historical background so you can better understand their use. While this is not a comprehensive list, the following historical paths can be found in Scotland; I have also included some information about where they feature in the routes in this book.

- **Roman roads:** the oldest known roads in Scotland were built by the Romans between AD 78 and AD 185. Parts of Dere Street still exist in the Scottish Borders near Jedburgh, included in route 3.
- **Medieval routes:** these routes are more widespread, but harder to trace. They were less engineered and were mainly formed by horses or humans over the centuries. For example, parts of the Southern Upland Way at Minch Moor, included in route 5.
- **Drove roads:** these were the 'highways' on which thousands of cattle streamed from the Highlands to the markets of the Central Belt each autumn. First to Crieff, then to Falkirk, and from there further across the border to England. Many routes in this book feature at least one drove road.
- **Kirk and coffin roads:** kirk is a Scottish word meaning church. Kirk and coffin roads were rights of way to churches or burial grounds. The cairns, where coffin bearers rested, can still be seen on some routes. Be mindful that some of

MAP KEY

 Route line

 Shortcut/optional route line

🏰 Historic site

⭐ Point of interest

🚲 Mountain bike centre

🌊 Notable river crossing

🍴 Food and drink

🛏 Accommodation

🏠 Bothy

🚆 Mainline railway

🚌 Public transport

⛴ Ferry port/crossing

£ Entry fee

these routes are steep. The section from Loch Lyon to Killin in route 19 is a former coffin road.

- **Military roads:** military roads were first built by General George Wade in 1724 to pacify and improve communication in the Highlands. His successor, Major Caulfeild, oversaw the completion of more roads, creating in total a network of more than 1,600 kilometres (1,000 miles). Many have since disappeared under tarmac and form part of Scotland's modern road network, but a good few remain as tracks. They are included in a number of routes in this book.
- **Turnpike trusts and Thomas Telford:** after the military roads, road building developed under the turnpike trusts. Thomas Telford was employed to build new roads in remote parts of the Highlands, and while there is no direct legacy from these for bikepacking, parts of Telford's roads can be found on route 19.

Most of the historic routes are marked with green signs erected by ScotWays. Today, there are over 4,000 signs scattered throughout Scotland, with some reminding people that a route is a right of way, while others tell the history and heritage of a path.

SCOTLAND'S GREAT TRAILS

Different to most bikepacking routes described in his book, Scotland's Great Trails (*www.scotlandsgreattrails.com*) are clearly waymarked with the symbol of a thistle within a hexagon. These are largely off-road routes, and most of them offer a choice of visitor services. Be aware that the quality of the trails can vary widely; there are no quality assessments before a route becomes a Great Trail. Many of Scotland's Great Trails have sections that are suitable for cyclists as well as walkers. Some routes, like the West Highland Way, have dedicated websites, while others have only a single page sitting within a council website. The routes on the left are suitable for cycling or bikepacking, but often with concessions, such as the need to lift your bike over gates.

SUSTRANS ROUTES IN SCOTLAND

There are approximately 2,644 kilometres (1,643 miles) of National Cycle Network (NCN) routes in Scotland, including 1,130 kilometres (702 miles) of traffic-free routes, which use a mix of railway paths, canal towpaths, forest roads, shared-use paths, segregated cycle lanes and redetermined rural footways. They are marked by blue signs, with the route number displayed in white writing in a red box; most routes in this book include at least one section of NCN. In recent years, Sustrans has created themed routes like the Caledonia Way (Campbeltown to Inverness), the Lochs and Glens Way (Glasgow to Inverness) and the Far North Way (Inverness to John o'Groats), which have their own brand identity. At times, these routes do follow roads, which means that following a review in 2018 of the whole network they no longer meet the strict criteria to be included in the NCN. So, waymarking on these routes is a mix of bespoke logos and Sustrans symbols. Sustrans, in partnership with VisitScotland, has also created a resource that lists cycling routes in Scotland. Find it online: *www.visitscotland.com*

BIKEPACKING SCOTLAND

The Bikepacking Scotland website lists a number of additional routes which were developed in partnership with destination management organisations, local councils or commercial partners. GPX files of these routes can be downloaded free of charge. A number of established Bikepacking Scotland routes are featured in this book; others, like the Reiver Raid and the Central Belter, can be found at *www.bikepackingscotland.com*

ROAD ITINERARIES

The creation of the North Coast 500 (see page 168) has led to a number of driving routes being promoted across Scotland. As you will often have to mingle with camper vans on singletrack roads in peak season, these routes are of only limited interest for bikepacking, but they can still provide good inspiration for you to map your own route. This book features an alternative North Coast 500 (page 161).

- Heart 200 – *www.heart200.scot*
- Kintyre 66 – *www.wildaboutargyll.co.uk/kintyre66*
- North East 250 – *www.northeast250.com*
- SnowRoads Scenic Route – *www.snowroads.com*
- South West Coastal 300 – *www.scotlandstartshere.com/swc300*
- The Coig – *www.ayrshireandarran.com*

MORE INSPIRATIONAL ROUTES

In addition to Scotland's Great Trails, Sustrans and Bikepacking Scotland routes, and the routes described in this book, there are more routes that either have their own website or simply exist as a GPX file which you can download for free or a fee/donation. Scotland has a very vibrant bikepacking scene, with new routes appearing on a regular basis. This is a list of routes that exist at the time of writing and which are not featured in more detail in this book.

- An Turas Mor – *www.anturasmor.co.uk*
- Borders 350 – *www.komoot.com/tour/558830131*
- Cairngorms Loop *www.cairngormsloop.net*
- Deeside Trail – *www.deesidetrail.com*
- Faultline Trail – *www.albannach.cc/thefaultlinetrail*
- Fife Pilgrim Way – *www.fifecoastandcountrysidetrust.co.uk/walks/fife-pilgrim-way*
- Great North Trail – *www.cyclinguk.org/route/great-north-trail-full-route-cape-wrath*
- Hebridean Way – *www.visitouterhebrides.co.uk/hebrideanway*
- Loch Ness 360° Trail – *www.lochness360.com*
- Kirkpatrick C2C, South of Scotland's Coast to Coast – *www.scotlandstartshere.com*

- Lomond Trossachs Loop – *lomondtrossachsloop.tumblr.com*
- River Tay Way – *www.pkct.org/pages/category/river-tay-way*
- The Pictish Trail – *www.bikepacking.com/routes/the-pictish-trail*

LEGALITIES

The routes in this book have been researched in respect of the current laws in Scotland and the wider United Kingdom. Please note that these laws can change. In the UK, cyclists are obliged to adhere to the Highway Code. Although no speed limits are applicable to cyclists, you can be charged with cycling carelessly or furiously. Cycling on a pavement is illegal unless it is also a cycle path. Helmets are not mandatory. At night, your bike must have white front and red rear lights (flashing lights are permitted), and it also needs to be fitted with a red rear reflector and amber pedal reflectors. You can be charged with cycling under the influence of drink or drugs.

THE SCOTTISH OUTDOOR ACCESS CODE

In Scotland, the Scottish Outdoor Access Code gives people the right to access to most land, including private roads, tracks and paths, for recreation and to get from place to place. This right is conditional on people acting responsibly. The main exceptions to the right are: people's gardens; farmyards (although access is at times possible – if in doubt, ask); and land in which crops have been sown or are growing (but you can use field margins as long as you avoid unnecessary damage to the crops). You can access golf courses (except greens and tees), but only to cross the area and without interfering with play. On golf courses, cyclists must keep to paths at all times. You are also allowed to cycle off-path, but you are encouraged to avoid going on to wet, boggy or soft ground, and churning up the surface.

Take care not to alarm farm animals, horses and wildlife, and do not endanger walkers and horse riders; give other users advance warning of your presence and give way to them on narrow paths. More information can be found at *www.outdooraccess-scotland.scot* and *www.dmbins.com/do-the-ride-thing*

ACCOMMODATION AND SHELTER

Scotland offers accommodation in all price ranges, from basic campsites to five-star hotels. The VisitScotland Cyclists Welcome scheme promotes cyclist-friendly accommodation. Providers offer extra facilities and services, such as drying facilities, secure bike storage and flexible dinner times, to make your stay even more comfortable. They display the Cyclists Welcome logo on their website and premises. Bike-friendly accommodation options are listed for each route in this book, and almost all of them have been personally tested by the author.

The following options for overnighting are specific to Scotland.

Bothies: a network of very basic and free-to-use shelters, some of which can be found on routes in this book. Originally accommodation for itinerant workers, most bothies are old cottages in remote locations a good distance from public roads. Expect nothing more than a wooden platform on which to unroll your mattress, and sometimes a fireplace. As they have very limited capacity, make sure you always take a tent or bivvy bag as alternative shelter. Most bothies are under the stewardship of the Mountain Bothies Association: *www.mountainbothies.org.uk*

Wild camping: Scotland's access rights extend to wild camping, as long as it is lightweight, and done in small numbers and for only up to three nights in any one place. You can camp wherever access rights apply, but please avoid causing problems for local people and land managers by not camping in enclosed fields of crops or farm animals, and keep well away from buildings, roads and historic structures. There is also one exception: seasonal camping restrictions and by-laws in the Loch Lomond & The Trossachs National Park mean that camping in certain areas of the national park is only permitted within campsites or with a camping permit between 1 March and 30 September.

Hostels: a good network of hostels can be found across Scotland, with many offering bike shelters, self-catering kitchens and a choice of shared or private accommodation. Scottish Hostels (*www.scottish-hostels. com*) is the organisation for independent hostels, bunkhouses, backpackers and activity accommodation providers, and Hostelling Scotland (*www.hostellingscotland.org.uk*), part of Hostelling International, provides youth hostel accommodation either run by the organisation or affiliated hostels.

BEASTIES

Scotland is a very safe country for bike-packing. Be mindful about the following beasties, but don't let them put you off a bikepacking adventure.

Adders: widespread across the Scottish mainland but rarely seen, the adder is the only venomous snake in Scotland. An adder bite can be very painful and cause a nasty inflammation, but it is really only dangerous to the very young, old or ill.

Midges: the Highland midge is a real nuisance from late spring to late summer. Female Highland midges are well known for gathering in clouds and biting humans, though most of the blood they obtain comes from cattle, sheep and deer. The best protection against midges is either cycling fast, or covering up by wearing long sleeves and midge nets when stopping. You can also use Smidge, available in many shops, a spray that works on all biting insects (including mosquitoes and ticks).

Ticks: ticks can be found across Scotland, and particularly in woodland, on moorland and in long grass. They can carry several diseases such as Lyme disease. Check yourself daily for ticks. The most reliable method for removing a tick without leaving any remnants in your skin is with a tick hook.

Coos: you will sooner or later meet a hairy Highland cow, one of the oldest cattle breeds in the world. Locals call them coos or beasties. Access rights extend to fields with farm animals, but remember that some animals – particularly cows with calves but also horses, pigs and farmed deer – can react aggressively towards people. Before entering a field with animals, check to see what alternatives there are, keep a safe distance and watch them carefully. Land managers are advised to keep animals known to be dangerous, such as bulls, away from fields crossed by core paths or other well-used routes. Often there will be a warning sign, but caution is advised even if there isn't.

FOOD/WATER/TOILETS

Each route features recommended places to eat. Eating locally means you produce less waste and support the communities you are travelling through. Vegan and vegetarian options are easy to find in Scotland, and in some places you can find fresh seafood. If you want to cook yourself, all four main types of camping gas canisters (screw-on, Easy Clic, pierceable and aerosol) are available. Screw-on canisters are the most common.

Although it is tempting to drink from streams, drinking water must be treated before it is safe to drink. If you want to fill up your bottles or bladder, there are currently 80 locations across Scotland where you can use the big and bright-blue Top up Taps provided by Scottish Water for free (*www. yourwateryourlife.co.uk*). Topping up at pubs

Oban Youth Hostel, Argyll (routes 12 and 13).

and cafes and so on is usually easy: just ask. Water purification (chlorine dioxide) tablets can help to sterilise water from natural water sources, but it will take around 30 minutes before you can drink the water. There are also water bottles and hydration bladders with water filters included – a good solution for more remote rides. Whatever you eat or drink, make sure you leave no trace and carry out all packaging.

Although they become rarer, there is still a good network of public toilets across Scotland. Bothies don't normally have toilet facilities. It is good practice to carry a trowel and do your business well away from any natural water courses.

WEATHER

Scotland's climate is milder than what you might expect from its latitude. The weather can often be completely different in various parts of the country. Precipitation is greatest in the mountainous areas of the west, as prevailing winds, laden with moisture from the Atlantic Ocean, blow from the south-west. Easterly winds are common in winter and spring, when cold, dry continental air encircles the east coast. The west tends to be milder in winter, with less

frost and with snow only at higher altitudes.

Scotland's weather can be extremely changeable. The average rainfall is the highest in summer, so spring and autumn are the best months for bikepacking. Don't rely on the weather forecast: it is best to pack for all conditions. That said, you are unlikely to have a snowstorm in summer. The wind chill, especially with easterly winds, can have a big impact on the temperature. The best weather forecasts come from the Mountain Weather Information Service (*www.mwis.org.uk*) and the Norwegian Meteorological Institute (*www.yr.no*).

DEER STALKING

Deer stalking is an essential part of sustainable deer management in Scotland and takes place during the stag stalking season, between 1 July and 20 October, and the hind stalking season, between 21 October and 15 February. In remote areas, you should ensure that you seek information on where stalking might be taking place, and avoid crossing land off the paths. Stalking does not normally take place on Sundays. The Heading for the Scottish Hills service (see *www.outdooraccess-scotland.scot*) helps you find out where stalking is taking place during the stag stalking season.

PLANNING YOUR SCOTTISH ADVENTURE

PICK YOUR ROUTE

This book offers a wide spectrum of routes; take your time and choose a ride that's right for you. If you are in a particular region featured in this book, your choice might be influenced by the nearest available route. Please read the descriptions carefully and decide if the route suits your expectations, riding ability or bike choice. The routes are either circular or point-to-point rides. Don't overestimate the distance you want to cycle in a day. Plan enough time for stops, and allow time for when things go wrong – like needing to fix a puncture.

CHOOSE YOUR BIKE

The different routes in this book are suitable for the following types of bikes.

Road bikes: skinny tyres, drop bars.
Gravel bikes: wider tyres, drop or flat bars.
Mountain bikes: even wider tyres, flat bars, optional suspension.

PREPARE YOUR BIKE

Make sure you clean and service your bike at regular intervals. How often will depend on your bike, the amount of riding you do and the conditions you ride in. Please clean your bike properly before and after you ride. If you are not confident maintaining your bike, I recommend booking a service at your local bike shop well in advance: don't rush to a shop on the day before you want to set off.

If you need help while you are on an adventure, the nearest bike shops are listed for each route. Some accommodation providers also have basic facilities that allow you to carry out simple repairs. It's worth learning the basics of maintenance, as some of the routes are very remote and you might be required to perform the following basic maintenance and fixes yourself:

- Checking and lubricating the chain.
- Removing the front and rear wheels.
- Replacing or repairing an inner tube, or, if tubeless, plugging a small hole in a tyre.
- Knowing how to place a tyre boot.
- Fixing a chain with chainlinks.
- Replacing brake pads.
- Adjusting brakes.
- Carrying out basic gear adjustments.
- Tightening or replacing a cleat.
- Tightening bolts properly.

GAELIC PLACE NAMES

Scottish Gaelic is a Celtic language, mainly spoken in the Highlands and islands of western Scotland. It was brought from Ireland in the fifth and sixth centuries AD and is now spoken by about 60,000 people. The following is a simple glossary of the elements from Scottish Gaelic most frequently found in the place names of Scotland, extracted from a guide that can be found on the Ordnance Survey website (www.getoutside.ordnancesurvey.co.uk).

SCOTTISH GAELIC

sabhainn – river
allt – burn or stream
beag – little
bealach – pass, col
beinn – mountain
camas – bay, harbour
caolas – narrow strait
càrn – pile of stones
ceann – head, headland
coille – wood, forest
coire – cirque, hollow in a hill
creag – crag, cliff
drochaid – bridge
dùn – fortress, castle
eas, easan – waterfall
feith – bog
gleann – glen (valley)
inbhir – mouth, usually of a loch or river
làirig – pass, col
loch – lake or fjord
lochan – small lake
monadh – mountain
rathad – road
sgòrr or sgùrr – sharp, rocky peak
srath or strath – wide river valley
uaimh – cave
uisge – water

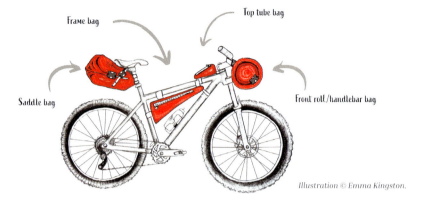

Top tube bag

Frame bag

Saddle bag

Front roll/handlebar bag

Illustration © Emma Kingston.

THE FOLLOWING LIST IS A RECOMMENDATION FOR WHAT TO WEAR ON YOUR BODY:

· Shoes (comfortable, ideally waterproof).
· Socks.
· Suitable cycling shorts/skorts or bib shorts or leggings/bib tights.
· Fast-wicking base layer.
· Jersey (short or long).
· Wind and waterproof jacket.
· Gloves.
· Helmet.

THE FOLLOWING ADDITIONAL PIECES OF CLOTHING ARE USEFUL IN SOME CONDITIONS:

· Shoe covers.
· Knee or leg warmers.
· Waterproof legwear.
· Arm warmers.
· Additional gloves (liners or outers).
· Cycling cap, beanie or skullcap.
· Buff.
· Gilet.
· Sunglasses.

Being able to carry out the tasks on this list will help you to fix likely problems yourself, and prevent you from potentially having to walk a long way. To be able to perform basic repairs, you should carry the following tools, spare parts and other kit on every ride:

- At least one spare tube.
- Multiple inner tube patches.
- At least two tyre levers.
- Multi-tool.
- Chainbreaker.
- Spare mech hanger.
- Tubeless repair kit with sufficient plugs.
- CO2 cartridge.
- Chainlink.
- Pump (with some duct/Gorilla tape wrapped around it).
- One spare cleat and bolts.
- At least one set of brake pads.
- Zip ties and tape.
- Small bottle of lube.
- Toothpaste wrapper or tyre boot.

Before setting off on each ride, you should always perform the M-check (a basic safety check) on your bike.

E-BIKE CHARGING

In partnership with Bosch, there are four free-to-use charging stations for e-bikes along the Caledonia Way: at Caledonian Canal Centre, Fort Augustus; the Ben Nevis Visitor Centre, Fort William; at Woodlands, Glencoe; and West Coast Motors Travel Shop, Oban. A further four charging stations can be found along the Highland Perthshire Drovers Trail: at Birnam Arts, Dunkeld; Escape Route Cafe, Pitlochry; Highland Safaris, Dull; and Comrie Croft, near Comrie.

WHAT TO WEAR

Although recommending specific clothing is beyond the scope of the book, here are some tips from almost a decade of bikepacking in Scotland. See the list opposite.

Wear what you are most comfortable in, and make sure you check the weather forecast before you head out; the longer you ride, the more likely you are to face changing circumstances. While Scotland enjoys a wide range of weather conditions, you are unlikely to experience extreme heat or arctic frost. Wearing multiple layers gives you much greater flexibility to adapt. In all seasons, try to avoid getting wet, either by sweating too much or from precipitation. Waterproofs are a must, even in summer, and a hood that fits over your helmet will be helpful. Synthetic clothing will dry quicker than wool-based clothing, but will also become smelly faster than natural fabrics.

WHAT TO PACK

In addition to a working bike and suitable comfortable clothing, you should carry the following on each ride, regardless of length:

- Mobile phone.
- GPS device or maps.
- Basic first aid kit.
- Emergency blanket.
- Water bottles or hydration bladder.
- Sufficient lights, with a backup for front and rear (for example, a head torch with red light function).
- Powerbank and cables to charge phone/GPS.
- Trowel and toilet paper.
- Down jacket and hat.
- Tools (as detailed opposite).
- Sunscreen.

Bags strapped to the handlebar, frame and saddle are the most common choices for bikepacking, so these have been used as examples. Make sure your bags are waterproof or have waterproof liners. What to pack is often a personal choice and differs depending on the kind of trip you are planning. The kit lists provided have been tried and tested on many trips, and are intended to help you think about your own list of items.

FRONT ROLL/HANDLEBAR BAG

- Beanie/skullcap.
- Gloves.
- Waterproof jacket with hood.
- Tent/bivvy.
- Inflatable mattress.
- Down jacket.

ACCESSORY POCKET

- Spork.
- Foldable cup.
- Foldable bowl.
- Knife.
- Lighter.
- Stove.
- Tea/coffee bags.
- Chlorine tablets.
- Trowel and toilet paper.

FRAME BAG

- Power bank and phone cable.
- Food for the day.
- Pump.
- Spare tube.
- Tools.
- Foldable backpack.

SADDLE BAG

- Long-sleeve top.
- Tights.
- Merino liner gloves.
- Warm socks.
- Underwear.
- Waterproof shorts.
- Sleeping bag.
- Micro travel towel.
- Emergency food.
- Gas canister.
- Personal hygiene products.
- Toothbrush and toothpaste.
- Head torch.
- Spare batteries.
- Other chargers and cables.
- Charging plug.

ScotRail Highland Explorer carriage on the Glasgow to Oban line.

GO BIKEPACKING!

TEST YOUR KIT

Small changes can make a big difference to your comfort on any cycling adventure. Find the saddle that suits you best, discover the food that makes you happy, check that your waterproofs really do keep you dry, and work out what's missing from your toolkit. Use the kit that suits you best. The more you ride, the more you will learn what works for you. Don't expect your first bikepacking adventure in Scotland to be perfect!

GETTING TO A ROUTE

To encourage you to leave your car at home, the routes in this book have been designed without the need for owning or renting one. Fourteen of the routes start and finish at either a railway station or a bus service that offers bike transportation. Another four start and finish less than two kilometres away from the nearest railway station or a bus service that offers bike transportation. For the remaining two routes (routes 02 and 16), you will need to cycle between 24 kilometres (15 miles) and 44 kilometres (27 miles) to the start or from the finish.

PUBLIC TRANSPORT

Bikes are carried free of charge on trains, buses and ferries in Scotland. However, some private ferry providers, like the Jura Passenger Ferry, are now charging extra for bikes. Most trains in Scotland are operated by ScotRail (*www.scotrail.co.uk*). The lowest number of cycling spaces on a train is two (on most trains), and the highest is 20 (on the Highland Explorer train from Glasgow to Oban and Mallaig). Booking a bike space is often required, and reservations can be made up to two hours before departure. Most local buses don't accept bikes, with the exception of Ember (*www.ember.to*) and Borders Buses (*www.bordersbuses.co.uk*), which have bike racks. Some Scottish Citylink coaches (*www. citylink.co.uk*) carry bikes and offer pre-booking a space, but only if the bike is in a bag or the drivetrain is covered. Some services carry bike socks. You normally save money when booking tickets in advance. Splitting up longer journeys is usually cheaper than booking a ticket for the whole distance. Make sure to either lock up or supervise your bike on the whole journey.

NAVIGATION

A separate GPS device and mobile phone are highly recommended when riding the routes described in this book. You can download all routes as GPX files (see page v) and sync them with the device directly, or with the help of a route planning platform like komoot. Make sure you always have a backup available, so if one device stops working, you can rely on the other. Sync the route to both devices before the ride, and, if possible, make the route available when offline, so you don't have to rely on a mobile phone signal. If one of your navigation devices stops working or runs out of battery, it is advisable to cut the route short and finish the ride in the quickest possible way, especially in remote locations. Carrying a paper map, compass and cue sheets as backup is highly recommended.

SAFETY

Do not rely on a single form of navigation, or having mobile phone signal (see Navigation, opposite, for more advice). Always carry a mobile phone to alert emergency services in the event of an accident. Phone signal may be intermittent, particularly in remote or mountain areas. A satellite GPS messenger is a valuable addition if you are planning to ride in very remote regions.

On your mobile phone, you can dial **999** to reach the police, fire and ambulance departments. Along the coastal areas, this number will also put you in touch with Britain's voluntary coastguard rescue service, the Royal National Lifeboat Institution. Calls are free from any public or private phone, but they should only be made in real emergencies.

Emergency services can also be contacted by text message, useful if you have low battery or intermittent signal. Although primarily aimed at deaf and speech-impaired people, EmergencySMS is available to anyone. Check if your service provider supports it. You can register by sending an SMS message 'register' to **999**. **Do it now** – it could save yours or someone else's life. EmergencySMS should only be used when voice call contact with emergency services is not possible. *www.emergencysms.net*

Mobile phones also let you store a medical ID which will help emergency services with the basic information. **Make sure it is up to date.**

Mountain and other countryside rescue services in Scotland are provided as part of national emergency services and by voluntary organisations. Organisations such as Scottish Mountain Rescue are charitable organisations, financed by public donation and reliant entirely on volunteers.

In the event of needing to call for rescue, prepare the following information:

- **Your name:** normally you are asked your full name, and sometimes your address, to identify you. Your mobile number will show on the emergency operator's screen, but you may be asked to confirm it.
- **Where you are:** make sure you know how to locate your coordinates using your mobile phone or smartwatch. The free apps **OS Locate** and **what3words** are fast and highly accurate means of pinpointing your exact location.
- **Phone number:** if you are low on battery, tell the operator and provide an alternative phone number of another group member.
- **What occurred:** detail the event that occurred in terms of numbers involved, their ages, and injuries and how they were sustained. Provide any detail you feel pertinent, such as fractures, medication or the time elapsed since the accident.
- **Rescuer details:** you may be asked various details that the rescue teams might require, such as local weather conditions.

Try and remain calm when providing this information, as your clarity and the quality of the information is of vital importance to the rescue team.

READING LIST

The following books either formed the inspiration for the routes in this book or offer further information:

- *Big Rides Great Britain & Ireland* edited by Kathy Rogers & Markus Stitz
- *Exploring Scottish Hill Tracks* by Ralph Storer
- *Gravel Rides Scotland* by Ed Shoote
- *Great British Gravel Rides* by Markus Stitz
- *Joining the Dots* by Lee Craigie (images by James Robertson)
- *Nothing to See Here* by Anne Ward
- *The Scottish Bothy Bible* by Geoff Allan
- *Scotland Mountain Biking (vols I & II)* by Phil McKane
- *Scottish Hill Tracks* by Scottish Rights of Way and Access Society
- *The Drove Roads of Scotland* by A.R.B. Haldane
- *The Hidden Ways* by Alistair Moffat
- *The Scottish Glens (various books)* by Peter D. Koch-Osborne
- *The Unremembered Places* by Patrick Baker

THREE ROUTES FOR FAMILIES

THREE ROUTES FOR E-BIKES

THREE ROUTES FOR SINGLESPEEDERS

BE RESPONSIBLE

Leave only tyre prints, take only photos and make a positive impact on the communities you travel through.

- **Keep it clean:** clean your bike and shoes before travelling to another region. Avoid transporting weeds and diseases like *Phytophthora ramorum*, which attacks larch trees and is present in South West Scotland and Argyll.
- **Pack it out:** do not leave any rubbish on trails – take it with you and, where available, use recycling facilities.
- **Toilets:** plan your day to take advantage of public toilets or facilities in cafes etc. If necessary, do your business well away from waterways and bury your poop and toilet paper with a trowel.
- **Share with care:** be mindful that you share the routes with walkers, drivers, horse riders, wildlife and livestock, and show respect. Never run stock: instead, pause and give them time to get out of your way. Make a big circle around any cows with calves, or change your route, if necessary. Always leave gates as you find them.
- **Respect our cultural heritage:** many places in Scotland have special spiritual and historical significance. Please treat these places with respect.
- **Climate change:** reducing carbon dioxide emissions is the most critical challenge of our time. You can do your part by taking public transport, sharing cars with others and avoiding flying.

BEYOND THE BIKE

While cycling is a huge part of the adventures described in this book, taking time off the saddle, relieving your muscles, tendons and pressure points, and enjoying the places your bike takes you to is as important. The Kennett Brothers from New Zealand (*www.kennett.co.nz*) describe bikepacking as a board game, with points scored for the following:

- **Live and learn:** check out interpretation panels on the sides of a track, visit a museum, talk to locals or hang out with other riders. Share your own stories and give people an opportunity to share theirs.
- **Chow down:** food is more than just fuel. Find your happy place at the great places to eat and drink along the way.
- **Mix it up:** make the most of the places of interest along the route. Take that wee detour and use the opportunities along the way. Some routes offer boat tours, kayak tours, walks or great places to swim.
- **Photo time:** stopping for a nice view and a picture slows you down and invites you to share it with others. That said, be mindful of what you share publicly. If you come across a secret bothy or a perfect campsite, keep it to yourself.

USEFUL WEBSITES

In addition to the websites mentioned in this book, the following are useful information sources to find bikepacking inspiration in Scotland:

- Bikepacking.com – www.bikepacking.com
- Cateran Ecomuseum – www.cateranecomuseum.co.uk
- Gravelfoyle – www.gravelfoyle.com
- Perthshire Gravel Trails – www.perthshiregravel.com
- Scotroutes – www.blog.scotroutes.com
- Self-Supported – www.selfsupporteduk.net
- South of Scotland – www.scotlandstartshere.com
- Visit East Lothian – www.visiteastlothian.org
- Wild About Argyll – www.wildaboutargyll.co.uk

SCOTTISH INSPIRATION

- Adventure Syndicate @adventuresynd
- Annie Le @a_girl_outside
- Brett DeWoody @brettdewoody
- Ed Shoote @Ilovemountains
- Galloway Cycling @gallowaycycling
- Huw Oliver @topofests
- Lee Craigie @leecraigie_
- Marcus Nicolson @marcusnicolson
- Mike Dennison @latitude_57
- Naomi Freireich @frikfrak74
- Neil Russel @handcycle_adventures
- Simon Willis @always_another_ adventure

Andrew Armour at the annual Dunoon Dirt Dash, held in September on the Cowal peninsula (route 11).

SOUTHERN SCOTLAND

01 AYRSHIRE ALPS, COAST & CASTLES

INTRODUCTION

This ride takes you through the beauty of the Galloway and Southern Ayrshire UNESCO Biosphere, which covers a large part of South West Scotland. On quiet roads and gravel tracks you can surprise yourself with a rugged and scenic coast, majestic forests, beautiful rolling hills and farmland, historic villages, and towns that inspired Rabbie Burns, Scotland's national poet.

THE ROUTE

The route starts at Ayr railway station – with frequent connections to Girvan in the south and Glasgow in the north – and then follows the A79 and B7024 south to Alloway. The village is best known as the birthplace of Robert (Rabbie) Burns and provides the setting for much of his poem 'Tam o' Shanter'. At Burns Cottage, the route joins the Poet's Path towards the Robert Burns Birthplace Museum (£), which is passed at the end of the loop. There are a number of Burns-related artworks to spot as you cycle along, the most noticeable being Kenny Hunter's Monument to a Mouse, made from cast iron. You cross a bridge and then join a section of cycle path on the former line of the Maidens and Dunure Light Railway. The South Ayrshire Paths Initiative is working on creating a multi-user path between Ayr and Girvan based on the railway route, similar to the section that has already been converted.

Your route continues on the cycle path, until a path on the right continues to a residential estate and Doonholm Road. The route joins the National Byway route to cross the A77 at Doonholm Park, and then follows this signposted route to Dalrymple. From here, a quiet road climbs to Guiltreehill and descends through the rolling hills of the Ayrshire countryside to Kirkmichael. Expect more beautiful countryside and more

ROUTE CONDITIONS
- Path: 8%
- Cycle path: 6%
- Road: 86%
- Recommended bike: gravel bike

Previous page: *From Moffat to Ae on Sustrans Route 7 (route 02).*

Clive Drummond on a gravel track in the Changue Plantation.

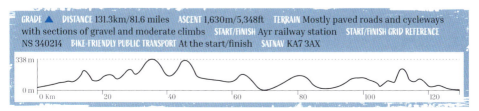

GRADE ▲ **DISTANCE** 131.3km/81.6 miles **ASCENT** 1,630m/5,348ft **TERRAIN** Mostly paved roads and cycleways with sections of gravel and moderate climbs **START/FINISH** Ayr railway station **START/FINISH GRID REFERENCE** NS 340214 **BIKE-FRIENDLY PUBLIC TRANSPORT** At the start/finish **SATNAV** KA7 3AX

338 m

0 m

0 Km · 20 · 40 · 60 · 80 · 100 · 120

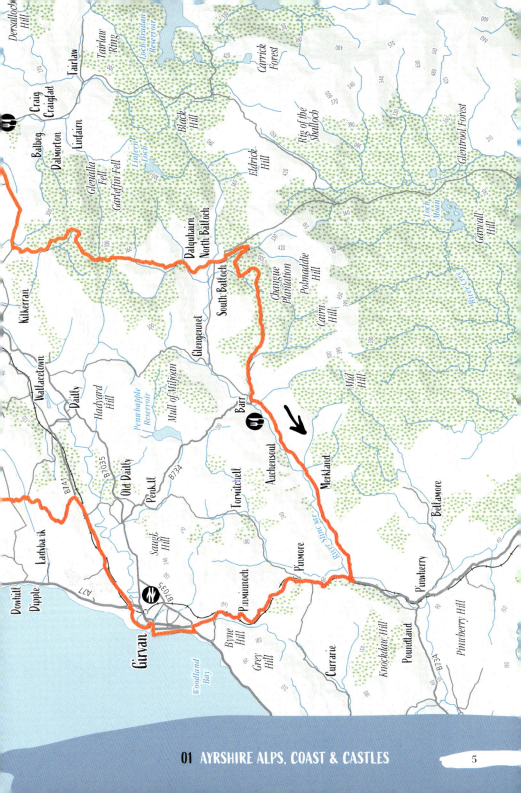

This route is good to ride all year round.

WARNINGS

The A77 is a major road with heavy traffic. Be careful when crossing, and if you need to shorten or alter the route, it's best to avoid this road.

FOOD AND DRINK

· Robert Burns Birthplace Museum, Alloway. T: 01292 443 700
· Kirkmichael Community Shop and Cafe, Kirkmichael. T: 01655 750 443
· Cafe The Buck, Straiton. www.facebook.com/cafethebuck
· Barr Community Store and Cafe, Barr. T: 01465 861 221
· Home Farm Kitchen, Culzean. T: 01655 884 455
· Harbour View Coffee Shop, Dunure. T: 01292 500 026
· The Anchorage, Dunure. T: 01292 502 826
· Turnberry Lighthouse, Turnberry. T: 01656 333 991

rolling hills while following the National Byway to Straiton. The route continues through the village first, and then back-tracks over farm tracks and a private road to a road that climbs steadily westbound and descends again to meet Sustrans Route 7. You continue into extensive forests, which are very typical for this corner of Scotland. The route reaches its highest point at the Black Hill of Garleffin, before it descends into more open moorland to South Balloch. From here, a nice off-road section takes you on wide and smooth gravel paths through Changue Plantation, reaching the highest point at Balloch Hill. The descent from here is awesome fun, and the small store in the village of Barr is a good place to stop for coffee and cake.

The route then undulates along the B734, a singletrack road alongside the River Stinchar, to Pinmore Bridge, where the A714 is joined, continuing through a beautiful wooded valley to Girvan. Girvan has a railway station and is an optional start or finish location. The route crosses the town and continues along the promenade, which is also the route of the Ayrshire Coastal Path, offering great views towards Ailsa Craig, the island which has long been the place where curling stones are quarried. In summer, it is home to 40,000 gannets. There are regular boat tours to this interestingly shaped rock, formed during the same period as the rocks on the nearby Isle of Arran, which is also visible on clear days.

At the end of the promenade the route joins the National Byway again, crossing the busy A77 and continuing steadily uphill on the B741 to Low Craighead. Here, another small road is followed, with more stunning views to Ailsa Craig on clear days. This and other sections are part of the Ayrshire Alps routes, which were developed by the local cycling club Ayr Burners Cycling. Watch out for stunning views to the coast while you descend to Turnberry, the village best known for its iconic golf course. The route makes a short detour to Turnberry Lighthouse, built in 1873, and the ruins of Turnberry Castle,

thought to be the birthplace of Robert the Bruce in 1274.

At Maidens, a series of rocks known as the 'Maidens of Turnberry' form a natural harbour, and the sandy beach with a grassy foreshore is a wonderful place to relax and enjoy the breathtaking scenery; on a clear day you can even see as far as the Mull of Kintyre. As with Turnberry, Maidens was one of the stations on the Maidens and Dunure Light Railway from Ayr to Girvan. Follow the road through the caravan park to enter the grounds of Culzean Castle (£) on the Ayrshire Coastal Path. Perched on the Ayrshire cliffs, the castle was designed by Robert Adam in the late 18th century; it once also decorated the back of a £5 note issued by the Royal Bank of Scotland. After following a series of tracks and roads through the country park, you'll reach the A719, and soon afterwards one of Scotland's oddest bits of road, the Electric Brae. Due to an optical illusion, freewheeling vehicles – and bicycles! – appear to be drawn uphill. Soon after, you reach Dunure, a small coastal village and a filming location for *Outlander*. Another ruined castle in a clifftop setting, a scenic former fishing harbour with a nice pub and cafe make Dunure a great location to rest for a while.

At Fisherton, the route joins the A719 to Genoch Farm. From here, the last proper climb follows Sustrans Route 7 over by Brown Carrick Hill. You'll be rewarded with amazing views from the top, and a sweeping downhill to Sauchrie. Sauchrie House was home to John Loudon McAdam, a Scottish civil engineer and road-builder who invented the process of 'macadamisation' for building roads with a smooth hard surface, which 'paved' the way for modern roads. Shortly afterwards, the route continues on the B7024 to Alloway, passing the Burns Monument and Birthplace Museum. From here, the Burton cycle track is joined to Doonfoot, where the route meets Sustrans Route 7. This quiet cycle path takes you along the waterfront first, and then on a succession of roads back to Ayr railway station.

ACCOMMODATION
· Various Airbnbs in the area – www.airbnb.co.uk
· Mercure Hotel, Ayr. T: 01292 844 299

OTHER ROUTES NEARBY
· Sustrans National Cycle Network Route 7 – www.sustrans.org.uk
· National Byway – www.thenationalbyway.org
· Ayrshire Alps routes – www.ayrshirealps.org

BIKE SHOPS AND HIRE
· Carrick Cycles, Ayr (shop). T: 01292 269 822
· Biosphere Bikes, Girvan (hire) – www.biospherebikes.com

VIDEO INSPIRATION

L–R: *Former railway bridge; Burns Cottage in Alloway; Culzean Castle.*

02 BORDERS TO COAST

INTRODUCTION

The Scottish Coast to Coast (C2C) route was launched in 2014 and links Annan on the Solway Firth with South Queensferry on the Firth of Forth. This is a variation of that route, starting in the Scottish Borders town of Peebles and finishing at the mouth of the River Dee in Kirkcudbright, one of Scotland's most vibrant arts communities. Along the route you can marvel at the Devil's Beef Tub, a dramatic hollow in the hills near Moffat, and the beautiful countryside that inspired Kirkpatrick Macmillan, widely credited as the inventor of the pedal-driven bicycle.

THE ROUTE

This route starts on the High Street of Peebles, best known for the nearby mountain bike trails at Glentress and the annual Tweedlove bike festival, and well-connected by bus with Edinburgh. Note that although the X62 service from Borders Buses has bike-friendly buses, be prepared to wait, and it's best to board at the Edinburgh bus station terminus. The route can be extended by cycling the whole Scottish C2C route, which is signposted from the Forth Bridge in Edinburgh to Annan on the Solway Firth.

Start your adventure by following the High Street and then crossing the River Tweed to head south, continuing on the Borderloop route past the Cademuir Plantation. The route skirts around Cademuir Hill, following the route of the John Buchan Way, a trail that connects Peebles and Broughton and celebrates the author of *The Thirty-Nine Steps*, a well-known adventure novel. Shortly before crossing the Tweed again, the route leaves the quiet tarmac roads for a path in the forest to Lyne Station, which served the village of Lyne from 1864 to

ROUTE CONDITIONS

- Path: 17%
- Cycle path: 9%
- Road: 74%
- Recommended bike: gravel bike

On a gravel track near Stanhope.

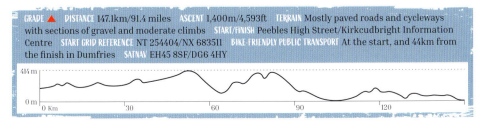

GRADE ▲ DISTANCE 147.1km/91.4 miles ASCENT 1,400m/4,593ft TERRAIN Mostly paved roads and cycleways with sections of gravel and moderate climbs START/FINISH Peebles High Street/Kirkcudbright Information Centre START GRID REFERENCE NT 254404/NX 683511 BIKE-FRIENDLY PUBLIC TRANSPORT At the start, and 44km from the finish in Dumfries SATNAV EH45 8SF/DG6 4HY

414 m

0 m

0 Km   30   60   90   120

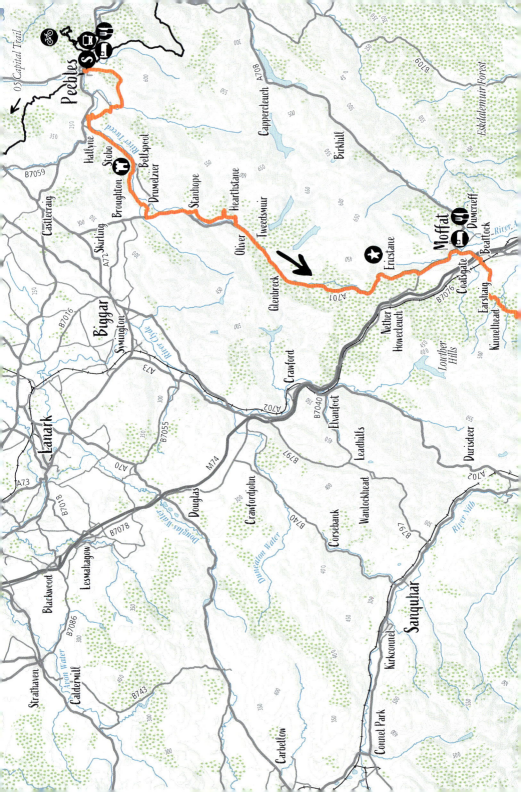

This route is good to ride all year round.

Be mindful that the section between Moffat and Ae has no resupply points.

· The Cross Keys, Peebles.
  T: 01721 723 467
· The Moffat Chippy, Moffat.
  T: 01683 222 777
· The Frothy Bike Co., Dumfries.
  T: 01387 248 770
· Solway Tide Tearooms, Kirkcudbright.
  T: 01557 330 735

The annual Raiders Gravel event takes place in August and this route is a good way to travel to the event by bike.
www.raidersgravel.com

L–R: Path to Lyne Station; A701 at the Devil's Beef Tub; Sustrans Route 7 from Moffat to Ae.

1950 on the Symington, Biggar and Broughton Railway; much of this route follows this old railway, and then from Broughton onwards, the former Caledonian Railway from Edinburgh to Carlisle. From Lyne, the route joins the B712 to Stobo, with the possibility of a short detour to Stobo Castle, before leaving the B-road and continuing on a minor road. Shortly afterwards, you pass the Altar Stone, part of the Merlin Trail. The route soon leaves the Borderloop and crosses the Tweed before joining the B712 to Rachan Mill, where it rejoins the signposted Borderloop.

You can see the remains of the former Caledonian Railway line as you follow the River Tweed and head south into the hills of the Scottish Borders. At Stanhope, the route leaves the road to continue on gravel paths on the eastern side of the river. This is one of the best sections of the route, with gradual climbs and descents as well as great views. At Heartstane, the route recrosses the river and rejoins the A701, climbing steadily past Tweedsmuir through the hills. You approach the highest point of the route at Flecket Hill, and shortly afterwards a viewpoint offers amazing views over the Devil's Beef Tub, a deep, dramatic hollow formed by Great Hill, Peat Knowe, Annanhead Hill and Ericstane Hill. It was used by the members of Clan Moffat and later the members of Clan Johnstone to hoard cattle stolen from the English in predatory raids.

On the descent you will cross the Annandale Way, one of Scotland's Great Trails, and in the forest you can find the line

of a Roman road which ran north from Moffat to the site of a watch tower on Ericstane Hill. The route follows the A701 all the way into Moffat; the signposted Annandale Way is a good alternative if you would like to add some more off-road riding. The small town has everything from bike shops to accommodation.

The route follows the A701 to pass under the A74(M), and then continues on Sustrans Route 7, initially climbing steeply. The route overlaps on this section with the Southern Upland Way, another of Scotland's Great Trails. Shortly after Wester Earshaig, your journey continues on a wide gravel track through extensive forests all the way to Ae village. Following the Romans and Reivers Route – yet another Great Trail – this section has amazing traffic-free cycling. Founded in only 1947, Ae is one of the youngest villages in Britain, and is also home to a superb variety of purpose-built mountain bike trails.

Continue to follow Sustrans Route 7 on a quiet road over open farmland to Locharbriggs, and from here pick up a cycle path all the way into Dumfries, a market town nicknamed 'Queen of the South'. Dumfries is also the closest railway station to the finish, and an alternative to the route described here is to follow the Scottish C2C route to Annan on the Solway Firth.

From Dumfries, continue on cycle paths all the way to Cargenbridge, and then on the Old Military Road to Lochfoot. This section of the route is best described as undulating: you are never far from either a climb or a descent. Follow Sustrans Route 7 all the way into Castle Douglas, another small market town. At Carlingwark Loch, a small freshwater loch, the route continues on a small road to Rhonehouse and along the River Dee to Tongland. You'll finish in Kirkcudbright, a vibrant arts community with events, exhibitions and activities taking place throughout the year, and a lively fishing port. From here, it is possible to extend the route with the Raiders gravel route described in *Great British Gravel Rides*, named after the annual gravel event which takes place in August in Gatehouse of Fleet – a further 12 kilometres from the finish by bike.

ACCOMMODATION
- Peebles Hydro, Peebles. T: 01764 651 846
- Moffat Independent Hostel, Moffat (also offers packraft & bike rental). T: 07920 460 105
- The Selkirk Arms Hotel & Restaurant, Kirkcudbright. T: 01557 330 402

OTHER ROUTES NEARBY
- Raiders gravel – www.adventurebooks.com/gbgr
- Scottish C2C – www.richardpeacecycling.com
- Borderloop and Kirkpatrick C2C, South of Scotland's Coast to Coast – www.scotlandstartshere.com
- The John Buchan Way – www.scotlandstartshere.com
- Annandale Way, Southern Upland Way and Romans and Reivers Route – www.scotlandsgreattrails.com
- Sustrans National Cycle Network routes 7 and 74 – www.sustrans.org.uk

BIKE SHOPS AND HIRE
- Bspoke Cycles, Peebles (shop). T: 01721 723 423
- Moffat Outdoors, Moffat (shop). T: 01683 220 270
- Ae Café and Bike Shop, Ae (shop, hire). T: 01387 860 805
- The Frothy Bike Co., Dumfries (shop). T: 01387 248 770
- Galloway Cycling Holidays, Castle Douglas (hire, tours). T: 07756 047 464
- Wm Law, Kirkcudbright (hire). T: 01557 330 579

03 BORDERS THREE ABBEYS LOOP

INTRODUCTION

The massive Waterloo Monument on the grassy hill of Peniel Heugh and three iconic abbeys are the highlights of this route. Watch out for the pig playing the bagpipes while you pass Melrose Abbey, the stunning bridges that take you over the Tweed at Dryburgh Abbey and Monteviot House, and follow in the footsteps of the Romans on Dere Street or the infamous Border reivers that raided the Anglo-Scottish border from the late 13th century to the beginning of the 17th century.

THE ROUTE

The route starts at Tweedbank railway station on the Borders Railway, with frequent trains to Edinburgh Waverley. Sustrans Route 1 is followed along The Black Path before the route continues along the banks of the River Tweed. You are riding the Capital Trail (page 31) in the opposite direction, and also the route of the Borders Abbeys Way. Watch out for jumping Atlantic salmon – the Tweed is one of Scotland's best rivers to spot this species, which is in sharp decline. After a gate, a path climbs to a church, where the route crosses the grounds and continues on St Mary's Road past Harmony House to Melrose Abbey (£). Harmony House is home to the Borders Book Festival, held annually in June. The abbey in Melrose is one of the three abbeys that give this route its name, and also the burial place of King Robert the Bruce's heart. It is open to visitors, and you will find the burial spot marked with a commemorative stone plaque. Watch out also for the carving in stone of a pig playing the bagpipes.

In Melrose, the route joins Sustrans Route 1 again, crossing the busy A6091. After the crossing, the Sustrans route uses the old main road to Newton St Boswells. Now closed to traffic,

ROUTE CONDITIONS

· Singletrack: 7%
· Path: 36%
· Cycle path: 6%
· Road: 51%
· Recommended bike: gravel bike

Louise Chavarie at Lanton Woods.

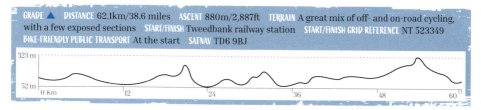

GRADE ▲ **DISTANCE** 62.1km/38.6 miles **ASCENT** 880m/2,887ft **TERRAIN** A great mix of off- and on-road cycling, with a few exposed sections **START/FINISH** Tweedbank railway station **START/FINISH GRID REFERENCE** NT 523349 **BIKE-FRIENDLY PUBLIC TRANSPORT** At the start **SATNAV** TD6 9BJ

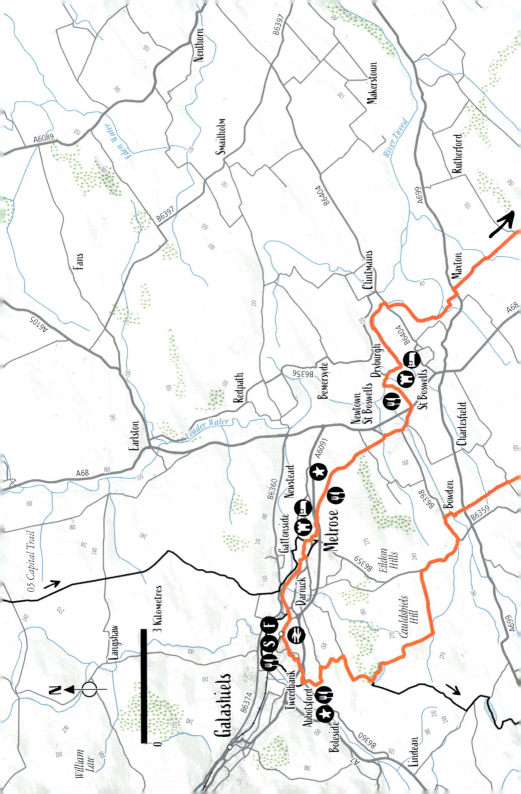

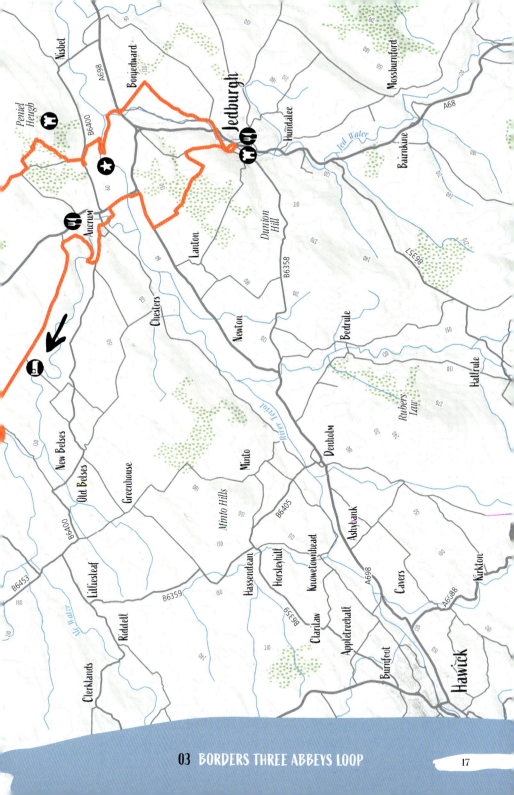

this is an enjoyable stretch to cycle, skirting around the north-eastern slopes of the Eildon Hills. You will meet the Borders Abbey Way at the Rhymer's Stone, a combination of memorial stone and viewpoint erected in 1929 by the Melrose Literary Society and marking the site of the fabled Eildon Tree. Under this tree, Thomas the Rhymer once took a fateful nap and was awakened by the Queen of Elfland. After kissing her, he spent seven years in the Land of the Elves before returning to his home in Earlston for another seven years, before disappearing for good.

The road continues to Eildon and through Newton St Boswells. Mainstreet Trading, one of Scotland's best bookshops and cafes, is only a short detour off the route in St Boswells. There is also a shop and a few other places to eat in the village. From Newton St Boswells, the route crosses the River Tweed on the Dryburgh Suspension Bridge. This footbridge was erected in 1872 after two other bridges had collapsed. It was a gift intended to allow the villagers of Dryburgh to worship at the churches in St Boswells. The Dryburgh Abbey Hotel is a good place to stop for food and accommodation. Dryburgh Abbey (£), the second of the three famous Borders abbeys along this route, is the final resting place of poet and playwright Sir Walter Scott, and is open to the public.

From Dryburgh, the route follows the Borders Abbeys Way along the banks of the Tweed to Mertoun Mill. This is a great stretch if you are looking for camping spots. The route crosses the Tweed on Mertoun Bridge – there are a few sets of steps leading down to the bridge – before joining the road first and then the signposted St Cuthbert's Way along the Tweed to Maxton. Along the way a few steps and wooden bridges need to be negotiated.

Passing the former Maxton railway station, which served Maxton from 1851 to 1964 on the Kelso Line, the route continues on a quiet road, climbing steadily to Pond Wood. From here a path to the left leads you up to Peniel Heugh, on which the Waterloo Monument stands. Visible from far afield, it dominates the views across the Scottish Borders. As with the bridge in Dryburgh, the original monument collapsed, and the current tower that commemorates the Battle of Waterloo was built between 1817 and 1824.

WHEN TO RIDE

May to November. Some of the tracks are popular with horse riders and get very muddy in the winter and early spring.

WARNINGS

The short section over Cauldshiels Hill is more technical than the rest of the route. This can be avoided by continuing on the road to Melrose.

FOOD AND DRINK

· Marmions Brasserie, Melrose.
  T: 01896 822 245
· Mainstreet Trading Company,
  St Boswells (detour). T: 01835 824 087
· Naked Sourdough, Jedburgh.
  T: 01835 862 787
· The Ancrum Cross Keys, Ancrum.
  T: 01835 830 242
· Ancrum Pantry, Ancrum.
  T: 01835 830 259
· Ochiltree's Cafe, Abbotsford.
  T: 01896 663 962
· Tempest Brewing Co. tap room,
  Tweedbank. T: 01896 759 500

ACCOMMODATION

· Burts Hotel, Melrose. T: 01896 822 285
· Dryburgh Abbey Hotel, Dryburgh.
  T: 01835 822 261
· Sandystones B&B, Sandystones.
  T: 01835 830 507
· Bowden House B&B, Bowden.
  T: 01835 824 571

L–R: The view from Peniel Heugh; wild camping on the River Tweed; Dryburgh Abbey; Dryburgh Suspension Bridge.

*One of the many quiet roads
in Scotland's south.*

You can enjoy the downhill path through the beautiful forest, before rejoining St Cuthbert's Way through the grounds of Monteviot House. Monteviot Suspension Bridge is another fine example of bridge building, before a singletrack along the southern banks of the River Teviot leads to Jedfoot bridge. A few steps lead up to the bridge. From here you will be cycling in the tracks of the former Dere Street, the Roman road which ran north from Eboracum (York), at least as far as the Antonine Wall in the Central Belt of Scotland. The John Muir Way (page 63) and the Falkirk Adventure Route (page 57) both pass the Antonine Wall. Portions of Dere Street's route are swallowed up by modern roads such as the A1(M), and other parts are followed by St Cuthbert's Way.

The signposts of the Borders Abbeys Way take you to Mount Ulston, with great views back to Peniel Heugh and across the rolling hills of the Scottish Borders, which inspired many writers, including Sir Walter Scott. At Woodend, the trail joins the road again and then continues on a cycle path into Jedburgh. The town is home to a ruined Augustinian abbey (£), the third abbey on this loop and founded in the 12th century. Jedburgh is also home to a free museum dedicated to Mary, Queen of Scots, set in a 16th-century tower house. There are a

number of places to eat, as well as shops and a service station, in this small Borders town.

Now, prepare your climbing legs as the next section up to Lanton Moor is steep. Where the road flattens a bit, follow a track into an extensive woodland which has plenty of good trails where you can extend the route if you like. The descent to Timpendean is pure joy and takes you past the remains of Timpendean Tower. After a short section on the A698, you'll cross Ancrum Bridge and join the Reiver Raid route to follow a number of smaller paths into Ancrum. This village on the Ale Water is a great place to stop; check out the local pub and shop for food and pints. The Ale Water Valley is a quiet and beautiful corner of the Scottish Borders, with a number of on-road and off-road cycling routes to explore further.

The route follows the road out of the village, and then joins a gravel path that skirts around Castle Hill and Broad Law to meet a road again at Scaw Knowe. You'll continue on tarmac to Birseslees, where the route continues on a drove road north to cross another road. A nice, but in winter very muddy, path takes you to the A699 and on to Bowden.

From Bowden, the route follows the road to Longleefoot, and continues on a gravel track to Lady Moss, a small loch on Faughill Moor. From here, a rough track is followed to the top of Cauldshiels Hill, the highest point of the route at 323 metres and commanding stunning views on a clear day. The downhill from here is steep, but soon you'll join a nice singletrack along the shores of Cauldshiels Loch, a popular outdoor swimming spot.

The route now follows the Capital Trail (page 31) in reverse to Abbotsford, the home of Sir Walter Scott. Both the cafe and museum (£) are well worth a visit. To finish, a nice cycle path links Abbotsford with Tweedbank station. If you arrive on either a Friday or Saturday, you can celebrate your adventure with a nice beer in the nearby Tempest Brewing Co. tap room.

THE
CENTRAL BELT

04 GO EAST LOTHIAN TRAIL

INTRODUCTION

Only a short distance from Scotland's capital Edinburgh, East Lothian provides the right ingredients for bikepacking journeys for all ages. The Go East Lothian Trail is perfect for families, for microadventures after work, or simply as an easy introduction to bikepacking in Scotland in all seasons, without compromising on anything that makes a good adventure.

THE ROUTE

Starting at the Scottish Seabird Centre in North Berwick, a vibrant harbour town with great beaches and an eclectic mix of shops and cafes, the route follows the road eastbound along the beach before a short climb takes you into a caravan park. This is also the route of 'Explore Your Boundaries: East Lothian', described in *Great British Gravel Rides*, but in reverse. The next section runs on the busy A198 and overlaps shortly with the John Muir Way (JMW) cycling route to Canty Bay, with views towards the magnificent Bass Rock, the world's largest colony of northern gannets.

After the section on the public road, the trail continues after Auldhame on a private road, taking you past Tantallon Castle (£), a ruined mid-14th-century fortress, to Seacliff Beach. From the car park, a small road climbs back up again, continuing past Scoughall to Peffer and Ravensheugh Sands; the dunes and beaches here are brilliant for walking. The route then joins a minor road at the car park at Tyninghame Links, which is the starting point for a variety of walking trails, before travelling a short distance on the A198 and then joining the B1407 towards East Linton for a short while. The Go East Lothian Trail continues on and off the JMW now. After crossing a ford,

ROUTE CONDITIONS
- Singletrack: 17%
- Path: 19%
- Cycle path: 10%
- Road: 54%
- Recommended bike: gravel bike

Previous page: *The Forth Bridge from South Queensferry (route 06).*

FamilyByCycle on the Go East Lothian Trail.

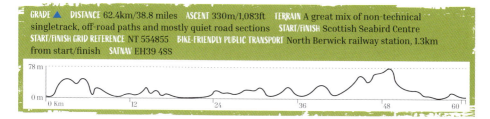

GRADE ▲ **DISTANCE** 62.4km/38.8 miles **ASCENT** 330m/1,083ft **TERRAIN** A great mix of non-technical singletrack, off-road paths and mostly quiet road sections **START/FINISH** Scottish Seabird Centre **START/FINISH GRID REFERENCE** NT 554855 **BIKE-FRIENDLY PUBLIC TRANSPORT** North Berwick railway station, 1.3km from start/finish **SATNAV** EH39 4SS

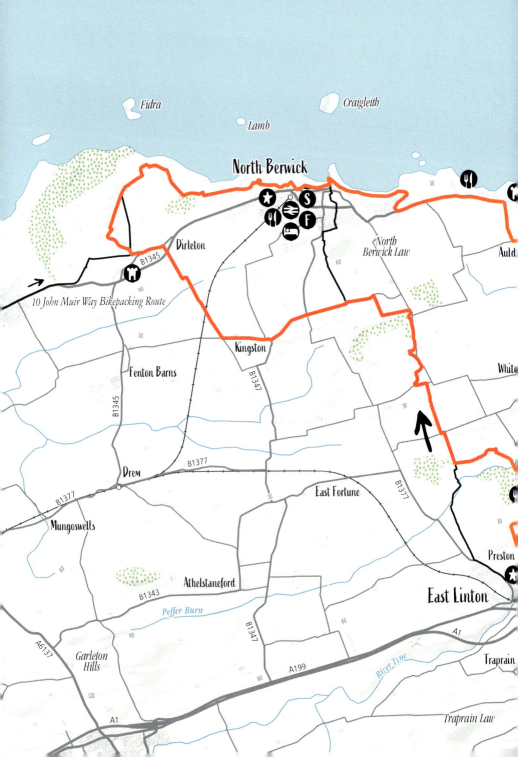

Fidra

Craigleith

Lamb

North Berwick

Dirleton

North
Berwick Law

Auld

B1345

10 John Muir Way Bikepacking Route

Kingston

Fenton Barns

B1347

White

B1345

Drem

B1377

East Fortune

B1377

Preston

Mungoswells

East Fortune

Athelstaneford

East Linton

B1343

Peffer Burn

B1347

A1

Traprain

A6137

Garleton
Hills

A199

River Tyne

A1

Traprain Law

L–R: Mark Beaumont cycling with a view to Bass Rock near Auldhame; coast near Tyninghame; anti-tank barriers at Hedderwick Sands.

the route leaves the signposted route and joins the A198 again. It continues on a rough gravel track on the right along the JMW to Hedderwick Sands. You'll cycle past a wetland on your left and concrete constructions on the right – anti-tank barriers during World War II.

After crossing a wooden bridge, the route follows a sandy track through a pine forest and past the popular East Links Family Park. From here, the Go East Lothian Trail continues on a track along the Biel Burn, before joining Sustrans Route 76 through Belhaven and into Dunbar, the birthplace of explorer, naturalist and influential conservationist John Muir. Diverting from the Sustrans route, continue on Belhaven Road and on to Dunbar High Street. John Muir's Birthplace, a small museum and centre for study and interpretation of the work of John Muir, is only a short detour away.

The route passes Dunbar railway station – a good alternative start if you are travelling from the south – and follows a cycle path, before crossing Lochend Road and continuing on a smooth gravel trail through the forest and past residential areas. Shortly after exiting the forest, the route picks up a gravel path alongside the A1 for a short section, before continuing on a minor road to West Barns, and from here on Sustrans Route 76 to Knowes. Here the route joins the JMW on a trail alongside the River Tyne. This trail can become muddy in wet conditions, but it otherwise offers superb riding to Preston Mill. A picturesque mill with waterwheel, millpond and doocot, it was used as a location in *Outlander*.

After East Linton, the route follows the B1407 for a short section and then a small private road to Smeaton Nursery. After a section of smooth gravel track, the route rejoins the JMW for a short while to Binning Wood. The next turn-off on the left, opposite the car park, is easy to miss, so take extra care. After passing through a gate, the route follows a walking path through Oak Wood, crossing the Peffer Burn to the right and passing a small loch to the left. The route takes a right turn at a country house, and then follows a farm track to join the John Muir Way after a few hundred metres. This section can get very muddy when wet.

Continue north on the JMW to Craigmoor Wood, one of the best parts of the route, where a flowy singletrack trail takes you through the forest, and then on a trail through a field towards North Berwick Law. The route then joins a small road to the left, which merges on to the B1347 to Kingston. You continue past Kingston Cottages to Dirleton. After a short section on Manse Road, a track through woodland starts at Dirleton Kirk and takes you to Yellowcraig. The playground here is very popular with kids. The route continues on the John Muir Way past Broad Sands (Yellowcraig Beach) into North Berwick, where it finishes back at the Scottish Seabird Centre.

BIKE SHOPS AND HIRE

· Law Cycles, North Berwick (shop, hire).
  T: 01620 890 643
· Ez-Riders, North Berwick (hire).
  T: 07407 039 747
· Belhaven Bikes, Dunbar (shop, hire).
  T: 01368 860 300

VIDEO INSPIRATION

05 CAPITAL TRAIL

INTRODUCTION

Although the Capital Trail does not venture far from Scotland's capital city, it does take you to some very remote and beautiful places, and has become a classic bikepacking adventure since its launch in 2015. This is an ideal ride if you want to get a real sense of bikepacking in Scotland without the logistical challenges of transporting your bike to the north.

THE ROUTE

The Capital Trail, the very first of a number of routes that Bikepacking Scotland has mapped over the last few years, starts on the Portobello Promenade. The closest train stations to the start are Brunstane and Musselburgh, both only a short ride away. The first section takes you along a traffic-free multi-user path along the beautiful coast of the Firth of Forth, an area steeped in industrial history and now home to many seabirds, including puffins. If you want to explore this part of Scotland further, both the John Muir Way (page 63) or From Forth to Fife (page 39) routes provide great incentives. The island of Inchkeith and the cliffs of the Fife coast dominate the view for a while, and various cafes and pubs invite you to stop. At the end of the 'Prom', the route joins the road and then continues along another promenade, this time in the small East Lothian town of Musselburgh.

From here the route follows the John Muir Way (JMW) first, and then Sustrans Route 76, before continuing along the banks of the River Esk to Whitecraig, joining Sustrans Route 1 before the village. A small – and, in summer, likely overgrown – path is a good shortcut to the cycle path. The Capital Trail continues on to the Carberry estate where it follows a network of singletrack

ROUTE CONDITIONS

- Singletrack: 21%
- Path: 36%
- Cycle path: 12%
- Road: 31%
- Recommended bike: mountain bike

Rich Rothwell descending on Gypsy Glen.

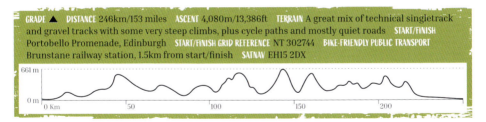

GRADE ▲ **DISTANCE** 246km/153 miles **ASCENT** 4,080m/13,386ft **TERRAIN** A great mix of technical singletrack and gravel tracks with some very steep climbs, plus cycle paths and mostly quiet roads **START/FINISH** Portobello Promenade, Edinburgh **START/FINISH GRID REFERENCE** NT 302744 **BIKE-FRIENDLY PUBLIC TRANSPORT** Brunstane railway station, 1.5km from start/finish **SATNAV** EH15 2DX

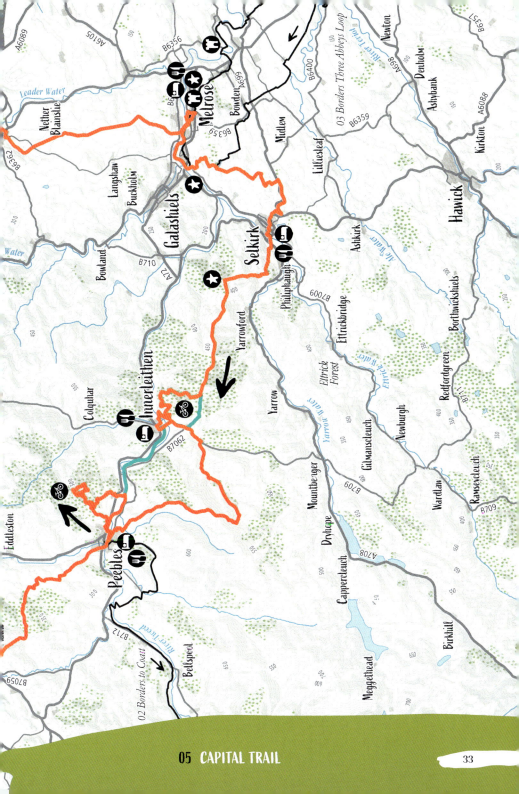

trails which can become muddy at times. The viewpoint on Carberry Hill is where Mary, Queen of Scots enjoyed her last few hours of freedom in June 1567. After a very short section on the road, the route follows a gravel track past a few houses with great views of the Firth of Forth to the north and the Lammermuir Hills to the south. A few lanes are followed from here and shortly after Elphinstone the Capital Trail joins Sustrans Route 196, better known as the Pencaitland Railway Walk. Ormiston, Scotland's first planned village, is a short detour away; along with the nearby village of Pencaitland, Ormiston is the last place where you can stock up with food until Lauder, 45 kilometres away.

One of the interesting features of the Capital Trail is that it takes you on small paths that are often even unknown to local riders. The next section of the route is exactly like this.

A mixture of singletrack and wider paths follows the Tyne Water, first through Winton Mains, and then, after crossing Spilmersford Bridge, through the grounds of Saltoun Hall. In West Saltoun, Sustrans Route 196 is followed for a very short stretch, before the Capital Trail continues through Saltoun Forest. Shortly after the woodland, there's a massive sign pointing you in the right direction; please follow the signposted route to Petersmuir Wood, from where a number of quiet country roads lead to Longyester. While the first section of the Capital Trail is relatively flat, you will enjoy some proper climbs from now on. The first steep climb follows at the northern end of the public road on the old road over Lammer Law towards Lauder. In past centuries, merchants and drovers would have used this old trade route which linked Haddington and Lauder, with wool carried northbound and grain southbound.

The route crosses the East Lothian boundary after Lammer Law, travelling through the vast landscapes of the heather-clad Lammermuir Hills. After another peak, Crib Law, you'll be treated to a steep and fast downhill, followed by an even steeper uphill. This is where the route overlaps with the Explore Your Boundaries: East Lothian route, described in *Great British Gravel Rides*. Once the top of this climb is reached, the route follows a combination of wide wind farm tracks and takes you to a small private shooting hut next to the Whalplaw Burn. In summer this is a fun section, with a few stream crossings to keep you refreshed on warm days; in winter, this part of the route will be very wet and muddy. At Longcroft, the route joins a quiet public road which leads to the A697. And at Drummonds Hall, the route meets the Southern Upland Way, one of Scotland's Great Trails, and continues through a beautiful woodland and past Thirlestane Castle (£) into Lauder, which is a good stop with cafes, a pie shop, shops and a service station.

From Lauder, the Capital Trail follows the route of the Southern Upland Way on a singletrack trail past Chester Hill, before a rather steep climb leads to Woodheads Hill. You can enjoy a bit less climbing now while rolling south through the hilly landscape typical of the Scottish Borders. A fast descent towards Melrose requires care, as this is also a popular walking route. After a rather gnarly trail along the banks of the River Tweed, you reach the small Borders town of Melrose, with its partly ruined abbey (£), said to be the burial place of Robert Bruce's heart. The town has excellent cafes and restaurants, and also hosts an annual book festival that is one of the best in Britain. For an extension to this route, check out the Borders Three Abbeys Loop (page 15).

From Melrose, the route follows the Borders Abbeys Way along the banks of the Tweed, where you might be lucky enough to spot Atlantic salmon jumping out of the water. Abbotsford, the home of Sir Walter Scott, is another great place to stop for coffee or a visit to the museum in the house (£). (If you'd like to split the Capital Trail into two adventures, you can follow the signposted Abbotsford Link and take the train back to Edinburgh from Tweedbank station.) The route climbs on quiet lanes to Cauldshiels Loch and on more rugged farm tracks past White Law to meet the road again at Lindean Moor. After a great path along the shore of Lindean Loch, the path gets rougher as it climbs towards the A699, on which the route continues until Selkirk Golf Club, where the Capital Trail follows the Borders Abbeys Way again for a short section before descending into the Borders town of Selkirk.

Stocking up on food here is a good idea, as the next section of the route is yet again remote, and also very exposed.

NAVIGATION

The path from Glenshiel Banks is very vague: be careful in low visibility. Navigation on the higher parts of the route can also be challenging in low visibility.

WHEN TO RIDE

The Capital Trail is best ridden between April and November – the days are longer and some sections can become very muddy in the depths of winter.

WARNINGS

The trails at Glentress are often used for events in spring and summer, so be prepared to avoid these if necessary. Some of the descents are steep and very loose: take extra care here.

FOOD AND DRINK

- The Espy, Portobello. T: 0131 669 0082
- Firebrick Bakery, Lauder. T: 01578 722 233
- Marmions Brasserie, Melrose. T: 01896 822 245
- Thai Valley Restaurant, Selkirk. T: 01750 778 174
- No1 Peebles Road, Innerleithen. T: 01896 209 486
- Loulabelles, Innerleithen. T: 01896 830 374
- The Cross Keys, Peebles. T: 01721 723467
- Olde Toll Tea House, West Linton. T: 07340 828 665
- The Fishmarket, Newhaven. T: 0131 552 8267

L–R: *On the Cross Borders Drove Road; the lone Bikepacking Scotland signpost near Saltoun Wood; woodland near Lauder.*

WATER

Note there are some long sections between opportunities to buy food or where it's difficult to obtain water, such as between Ormiston and Lauder, and north of Selkirk.

ACCOMMODATION

· Burts Hotel, Melrose. T: 01896 822 285
· The County, Selkirk. T: 01750 705 000
· Cleikum Mill Lodge, Innerleithen.
  T: 07790 592 747
· Peebles Hydro, Peebles. T: 01764 651 846

OTHER ROUTES NEARBY

· Borders to Coast (page 9), Borders Three Abbeys Loop (page 15), From Forth to Fife (page 39) and John Muir Way Bikepacking Route (page 63).
· Explore Your Boundaries East Lothian and Mór Tweed Valley Gravel – www.adventurebooks.com/gbgr
· Southern Upland Way and Borders Abbeys Way – www.scotlandsgreattrails.com
· Pentland Way – www.pentlandfriends.org.uk
· Kirkpatrick C2C, South of Scotland's Coast to Coast – www.scotlandstartshere.com

L–R: Josh Ibbett and the author at the Three Brethren; Gypsy Glen between Traquair and Peebles.

Surprisingly (for Scotland), natural water sources are in short supply as you climb up from Ettrick Water towards the Three Brethren. The higher you climb, the more rugged the trails get, and be prepared to lift your bike over a stile at Tibbie Tamson's Grave. The views as you approach the Three Brethren are spectacular; this is one of the many postcard motifs you'll find along the route. At a height of 465 metres, the Three Brethren cairns mark the boundaries of the estates of Buccleuch, Yair and Selkirk Burgh. From here, the route continues on the Southern Upland Way, with 360-degree views across the uplands of the Scottish Borders. The route undulates along the Old Drove Road and passes a few hills on a mixture of singletrack trails and rough doubletracks. Instead of continuing on the Old Drove Road to Traquair (a good shortcut if you are pushed for time), the Capital Trail follows the Innerleithen XC route and then a wide and fast gravel track that eventually meets the road to continue into Innerleithen and then on to Traquair, home to Scotland's oldest inhabited house. Innerleithen and nearby Peebles are both mountain bike meccas.

If you are no fan of pushing bikes and can live with missing one of the best natural downhills in Scotland, then the next section of the Capital Trail can be substituted by taking the flat Tweed Valley Railway Path to Peebles. However, the Capital Trail follows a small road into Glen Estate, where it overlaps with another route from *Great British Gravel Rides*, Mór Tweed Valley gravel. After a small cottage at Glenshiel Banks, the route follows a vague track through the heather to meet a wider path on the flanks of Stake Law, and continues to the highest point at Birkscairn Hill. Shortly after, the route meets the Cross Borders Drove Road and undulates on the Gypsy Glen MTB route to Kirkhope Law. The name Gypsy Glen originates from the camping site used by Travellers on the descent to Peebles. This is an amazing downhill, following a track bounded by drystone

dykes into another buzzing Borders town.

The next section of the Capital Trail gives you a taste of the Glentress mountain bike trails; they can get very busy on weekends and are often closed during events. If this is the case, simply continue through Peebles, where after the Rosetta campsite the route follows the Cross Borders Drove Road across the Meldons all the way to Romannobridge. This section will test your legs again but offers wonderful scenery. Be prepared to cross a field with loads of cows who are often in residence.

From Romannobridge, the Capital Trail follows the B7059 to West Linton and continues to Carlops at the foot of the Pentland Hills. After the village, watch out for a small path which eventually meets a small road to Nine Mile Burn. A grassy and at times unrideable climb takes you on the Pentland Way past Monks Rig to a small pass, with the highest peak in the Pentlands, Scald Law (579 metres), to your right. There are a number of stiles along this section that require the lifting of bikes. The descent from here to Bavelaw Castle is fast and fun. From here, a great track takes you to Loganlee and Glencorse reservoirs, and over the Maiden's Cleugh to Currie and on into Edinburgh.

Like the beginning of the route, the last section of the Capital Trail follows lesser-known trails: from Juniper Green past Heriot-Watt University to Cammo Estate. You'll pass the distinctive Cammo Tower, built in the early 19th century to supply water to nearby Cammo House. The house, now a ruin, is thought to be the inspiration for House of Shaws in Robert Louis Stevenson's 1886 novel *Kidnapped*. After passing through the estate, the route continues along the River Almond to Cramond, where it follows cycle paths along Edinburgh's shore through Silverknowes, Granton, Trinity, Newhaven and Leith back to the start. If seafood is your thing, make a short detour to The Fishmarket in Newhaven.

BIKE SHOPS AND HIRE

- Biketrax Edinburgh (shop, hire).
  T: 0131 228 6633
- ProjektRide, Edinburgh (shop, hire).
  T: 0131 374 5324
- Velow Bikeworks, Edinburgh (shop) –
  www.velow.cc
- BG Cycles, Edinburgh (shop).
  T: 0131 657 5832
- Ace Bike Co, Musselburgh (shop).
  T: 0131 665 4468
- Hardies Bikes, Melrose (shop).
  T: 01896 823 332
- i-cycles, Innerleithen (shop).
  T: 01896 829 680
- The Bike Shop, Innerleithen
  (shop, hire). T: 07770 974 201
- Tweed Valley Bikes, Innerleithen
  (shop). T: 01896 831 429
- Alpine Bikes, Glentress (shop, hire).
  T: 01721 724 522
- Bspoke Cycles, Peebles (shop).
  T: 01721 723 423

VIDEO INSPIRATION

06 FROM FORTH TO FIFE

INTRODUCTION

Starting from Edinburgh, this route is ideal for a micro-adventure or a family bikepacking trip. En route, you will experience the history of the Firth of Forth, with its magnificent bridges, stunning woodlands and the beauty of two lochs.

THE ROUTE

Starting from Haymarket railway station, also a stop for the bike-friendly Ember electric bus service, your route first follows Sustrans Route 1/76 on to the Roseburn cycle path. The route leaves the Sustrans route at Craigleith and continues on another cycle path alongside West Granton Access, and from here on a cycle lane along the road to Forthquarter Park. Already visible from far afield, you'll now pass the Granton gas holder. Built between 1898 and 1902, it was part of the Granton Gasworks which served the city of Edinburgh and the surrounding district throughout the 20th century.

The route continues through the park, and just before the Silverknowes Esplanade a small singletrack to the left is followed on the edge of Craigroyston woodland. As an alternative, you can also follow the esplanade, which is joined after about a kilometre. The route continues on the esplanade to Cramond breakwater. Cramond Island, a tidal island in the Firth of Forth, is accessible through the breakwater at low tide; cycling to the island is not recommended.

From here, the route follows the first part of the River Almond Walkway, and then continues up School Brae, before heading back down to the River Almond Walkway along Peggy's Mill Road. The section in between has multiple sets of slippery steps, hence this short detour. The route meets Sustrans Route 1/76 again at Cramond Old Bridge over the River Almond, also

ROUTE CONDITIONS

- Singletrack: 28%
- Path: 16%
- Cycle path: 24%
- Road: 32%
- Recommended bike: mountain or gravel bike

Sandy and Charlotte Anderson at Carlingnose Point Nature Reserve in North Queensferry.

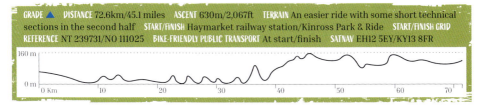

GRADE ▲ DISTANCE 72.6km/45.1 miles ASCENT 630m/2,067ft TERRAIN An easier ride with some short technical sections in the second half START/FINISH Haymarket railway station/Kinross Park & Ride START/FINISH GRID REFERENCE NT 239731/NO 111025 BIKE-FRIENDLY PUBLIC TRANSPORT At start/finish SATNAV EH12 5EY/KY13 8FR

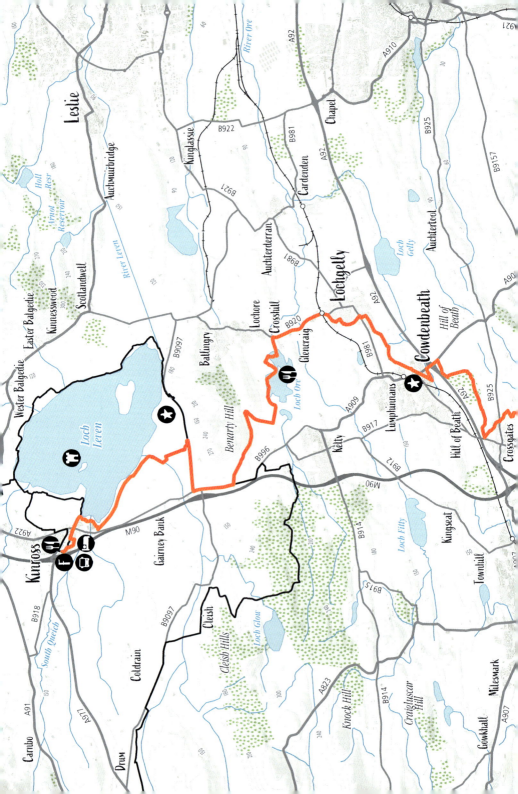

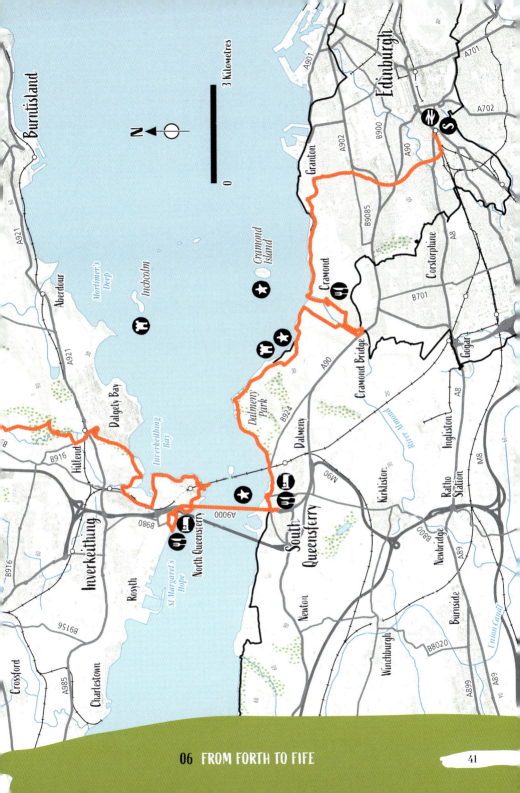

NAVIGATION

The route alternates depending on which side of the Forth Road Bridge is open for cyclists. Follow the signage.

WHEN TO RIDE

While the southern section to North Queensferry can be ridden all year, the northern section of the route can get muddy from November to April.

FOOD AND DRINK

- Cramond Bistro, Cramond –
  www.cramondbistro.co.uk
- Honey Pot Creative Cafe,
  South Queensferry –
  www.honeypotcreativecafe.com
- The Boathouse, South Queensferry.
  T: 0131 331 5429
- Manna House Bakery, South
  Queensferry. T: 0131 331 1661
- Rankin's Cafe, North Queensferry.
  T: 01383 616 313
- The Shore Grill & Fish House,
  North Queensferry. T: 01383 427 701
- Lochside Café, Lochore Meadows
  Country Park, Lochgelly.
  T: 03451 55 55 55 ext. 402258
- Unorthodox Roasters, Kinross.
  T: 07856 865 065
- The Court House, Kinross.
  T: 01577 351 020

The most famous of the Forth Bridges, from a small beach in South Queensferry.

the route of the John Muir Way walking route, which is followed from here through Dalmeny Estate; Dalmeny House (£) is open in the summer for guided tours. Once at the shore, you'll pass Hunter's Craig or Eagle Rock, a weather-worn carving of an eagle, dating back to the Roman occupation of Cramond. Shortly afterwards, where you pass a few houses, the route leaves the John Muir Way and continues on the Sustrans route to Dalmeny House, a Gothic revival mansion and home of the Earl and Countess of Rosebery. The house is open to the public in summer months. A little further along is the 13th-century Barnbougle Castle. Rebuilt in 1881 by the Victorian prime minister Archibald Philip Primrose, the 5th Earl of Roseberry, it is nowadays a popular wedding venue and filming location.

Passing through extensive woodlands you'll get great views of the Firth of Forth and Hound Point, the largest oil-export terminal in Scotland. Soon afterwards you'll see the Forth Bridge, the world's longest cantilever bridge and one of Scotland's UNESCO World Heritage Sites. It was also one of the world's first major steel structures and a milestone in the history of modern railway engineering. While you pass underneath the bridge in South Queensferry, you can get even more up close at Battery Road picnic area in North Queensferry. The best stop for a coffee is the small Honey Pot cafe right next to the route in South Queensferry.

If you want to explore the Firth of Forth further, or plan a visit to Inchcolm island with its former Augustine abbey, you can take a boat tour from Hawes Pier: both Forth Boat Tours and Maid of the Forth are great options. Along this route there are also information signs which are part of the Forth Bridges Trail, a circular trail which takes in the three iconic Forth Bridges and the communities of North and South Queensferry.

The route follows South Queensferry's High Street – you'll pass a number of shops and restaurants, and yet more interesting viewpoints from which to marvel at the bridges. A short loop takes you to The Binks, a rock formation that formed a natural jetty for the boats that once took passengers to the other side of the Forth to North Queensferry.

There's a sign right underneath the Forth Road Bridge to indicate which cycle path (east/west) is open, and the direction is given to access the path and the bridge. Once you have crossed one of the world's most significant long-span suspension bridges, the route makes a short detour to St Margaret's Marsh, a small saltmarsh, from where you'll get great views towards the Queensferry Crossing, the newest addition to the Forth Bridges, and the longest three-tower, cable-stayed bridge in the world.

The route then descends into the picturesque North Queensferry, which is usually much quieter than its southern equivalent on the other side of the Forth. Both the Town Pier and the Light Tower are remnants from the improvement of the former ferry service over the Forth in the early 19th century, which finally ceased when the Forth Road Bridges opened. Today, a small museum gives you a great insight into the history of this part of Scotland, before the route continues to Battery Road picnic area and past the Chapel of St James the Apostle to join the Fife Coastal Path and Fife Pilgrim Way through the Carlingnose Point Nature Reserve. The route skirts around the coast and passes an industrial estate into Inverkeithing. From here you can follow Ferryhill Road to North Queensferry railway station if you want to shorten the ride.

Continue on Sustrans Route 76, first through Inverkeithing before joining a singletrack trail past Prestonhill Quarry to Letham Hill Wood: a few steps must be negotiated at the entrance to this stunning woodland. The route descends into a residential area in Dalgety Bay and continues north on a cycle path. At Pargillis Bridge, the route continues through Fordell Glen and along some wide gravel tracks to Fordell. Just before the village there is a locked gate with pedestrian access through a kissing gate where you must lift your bike, before the route continues on a short section of singletrack trail and quiet roads to Coalcdgc.

From here tracks are followed towards Cowdenbeath, with a short section on the busy A909. Two stunning murals on Cowdenbeath's High Street are worth a short detour. The route follows a cycle path first and then a track that crosses a golf course to arrive in Lochgelly, where residential streets and paths are followed to the train station. From here the route continues on a cycle path next to the main road. The route continues through Lochore Meadows Country Park and on two busier roads and then joins the Loch Leven Heritage Path at East Brackley, continuing north to Kinross. Two big gates require you to lift the bike again, or you can also continue on the road to the RSPB information centre and cafe and join the route without the obstruction of a gate there. Arriving in Kinross, more roads and cycle paths lead you to the finish at Kinross Park & Ride, where frequent Ember bus services leave for Dundee or Edinburgh, and take bikes for free. Alternatively, the Discovering Perthshire's Heritage route (page 45) or the Lomond Hills gravel route in *Great British Gravel Rides* can extend your bikepacking adventure.

ACCOMMODATION

· DoubleTree by Hilton, Queensferry Crossing. T: 01383 410 000
· Orocco Pier Hotel, South Queensferry. T: 0131 331 1298
· Hawes Inn, South Queensferry. T: 0131 331 1990
· Travelodge, Kinross. T: 0871 984 6151

OTHER ROUTES NEARBY

· Discovering Perthshire's Heritage (page 45) and John Muir Way Bikepacking Route (page 63).
· Lomond Hills gravel – www.adventurebooks.com/gbgr
· Sustrans National Cycle Network routes 1 and 76 – www.sustrans.org.uk
· Fife Coastal Path – www.scotlandsgreattrails.com
· Fife Pilgrim Way – www.fifecoastand countrysidetrust.co.uk
· Forth Bridges Trail – www.theforthbridges.org

BIKE SHOPS AND HIRE

· Biketrax Edinburgh (shop, hire). T: 0131 228 6633
· Ryan's Bike Surgery, Inverkeithing (shop). T: 01383 420 777
· Sinclair Cycles Loch Leven, Channel Farm (shop, hire). T: 07753 708 934

VIDEO INSPIRATION

07 DISCOVERING PERTHSHIRE'S HERITAGE

INTRODUCTION

A motorway service station now occupies the site of the former Kinross Junction railway station, which served the burgh of Kinross from 1860 to 1970 on the Fife and Kinross Railway. This route retraces parts of the former railway which got swallowed by the M90, taking you past a stunning viaduct and two tunnels, before backtracking the routes of the drovers across the beautiful Ochil Hills. Good lights are recommended for the tunnels.

THE ROUTE

This route starts at Kinross Park & Ride, an Ember bus stop. Ember provides free bike spaces on its electric buses and it's therefore the best way to travel with your bike to Kinross from Edinburgh or Dundee. From the park and ride, the route follows a cycle path and then a quiet road through a residential area, and then crosses the High Street, also the route of Sustrans Route 775 which connects Kinross with Perth. Another small road takes you to the shores of Loch Leven and on to Sustrans Route 1. If you would like to enjoy a longer bikepacking adventure, it is possible to combine this route with the Lomond Hills gravel route in *Great British Gravel Rides*: that route travels in the opposite direction from here and meets this route again at Tarhill.

Loch Leven is a huge expanse of open water that mixes history and nature perfectly. As a nature reserve, it provides an ideal home for countless birds and the Loch Leven brown trout, famed worldwide for its flavour. From a historical perspective, Lochleven Castle, nestled on an island, is best known as the place where Mary, Queen of Scots was held prisoner for almost a year.

ROUTE CONDITIONS
· Singletrack: 17%
· Path: 24%
· Cycle path: 3%
· Road: 56%
· Recommended bike. gravel bike

WHEN TO RIDE
This route is best ridden from April to November, as paths can get muddy in the winter months.

Former railway viaduct at Glenfarg.

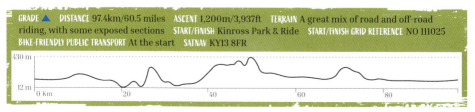

GRADE ▲   DISTANCE 97.4km/60.5 miles   ASCENT 1,200m/3,937ft   TERRAIN A great mix of road and off-road riding, with some exposed sections   START/FINISH Kinross Park & Ride   START/FINISH GRID REFERENCE NO 111025   BIKE-FRIENDLY PUBLIC TRANSPORT At the start   SATNAV KY13 8FR

430 m

12 m
0 Km   20   40   60   80

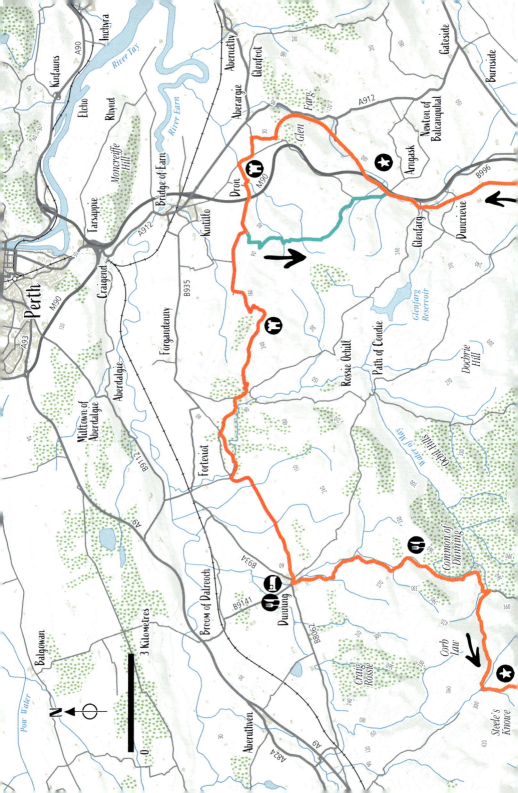

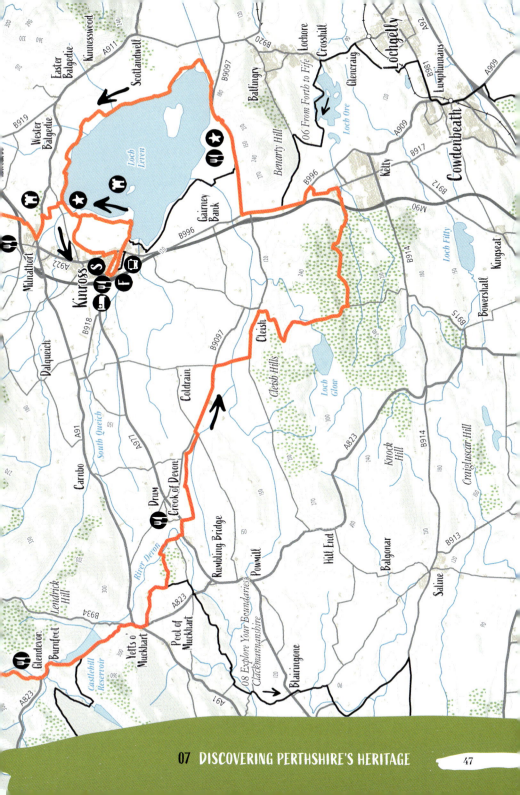

FOOD AND DRINK

· Unorthodox Roasters, Kinross.
  T: 07856 865 065
· The Court House, Kinross.
  T: 01577 351 020
· Heaven Scent Coffee Shop, Milnathort.
  T: 01577 865 577
· Kirkstyle Inn, Dunning. T: 01764 684 248
· Greenhill Farm Shop, near Dunning.
  T: 01764 684 601
· Tormaukin Hotel, Glendevon –
  www.thetormaukin.co.uk
· The Inn, Crook of Devon.
  T: 01577 840 207
· RSPB Scotland Loch Leven nature
  reserve. T: 01577 862 355

ACCOMMODATION

· Travelodge, Kinross. T: 0871 984 6151
· The Kirkstyle Inn, Dunning.
  T: 01764 684 248

OTHER ROUTES NEARBY

· From Forth to Fife (page 39)
  and Explore Your Boundaries:
  Clackmannanshire (page 51).
· Lomond Hills gravel –
  www.adventurebooks.com/gbgr
· Sustrans National Cycle Network
  routes 1 and 775 – www.sustrans.org.uk
· Loch Leven Heritage Trail –
  www.pkct.org
· Wallace Road and Cadgers' Yett –
  www.scotways.com/heritage-paths

BIKE SHOPS AND HIRE

· Sinclair Cycles Loch Leven, Channel
  Farm (shop, hire). T: 07753 708 934

L–R: *Corb Glen; lavender field at Loch Leven; former railway tunnel at Glenfarg.*

Your route follows the shore of the loch until Tarhill, easily recognisable by a car park. Follow a number of tracks to the A911, passing the ruin of Burleigh Castle en route. The route follows the road into Milnathort, where you can find a great cafe, but this can be very busy on weekends. From here, the quiet roads of Sustrans Route 775 lead to Glenfarg. This section travels through rolling countryside, with great views to the east of the Lomond Hills. After joining a path at the edge of Glenfarg, the route joins the B996 which can get busy at times. Around 500 metres after passing underneath the M90, you'll find a gravel path on your right. This is the former track bed of the North British Railway which closed in 1970; most of its route was used for building the M90 motorway. This section has survived, and along it you'll soon pass under a viaduct and through two tunnels. Each tunnel is about 500 metres in length (lights essential) and the surface is great for cycling. However, there are some sandy stretches and the route can get very muddy after you exit the first tunnel.

Continue on the former railway line until a track descends north at Kilknockiebank, following a small burn. You'll reach the road shortly afterwards and follow Sustrans Route 775 for a short stretch, before continuing on a quiet lane to Balmanno Castle, a moated tower house located in the hamlet of Dron. (If you are after a shorter day-ride, the Wallace Road, a heritage path, leads back to Glenfarg from here.) The main route continues on a small road to Glenearn, from where a very steep track climbs towards Glenearnhill. Your hard work is rewarded with commanding views north over Strathearn. Once you reach a ruined house, a short detour takes you to a fort that occupies the summit of Castle Law. The descent from the top is great, as you cruise deep into the heart of the Ochil Hills. The route from here travels south through the eastern part of the hills – which are clearly visible from as far afield as Edinburgh. The Explore Your Boundaries: Clackmannanshire route (page 51) provides another great bikepacking adventure in this area, but it is better suited to mountain bikes.

Shortly after Culteuchar, you are back on tarmac for a short stretch, before using a track through the grounds of Invermay and the Old House of Invermay to meet the road that continues to Dunning. This scenic Perthshire village has a shop, and a pub with rooms, and is your best bet as the main stop on the route. From here, the route climbs steadily southwards on the B934. After about 3.4 kilometres, a short detour takes you to Gray Stone, a standing stone in a beautiful setting.

Continue on the road for another four kilometres, passing a nice farm shop at Greenhill, before turning on to a wide track into the gravel heaven of Corb Glen. The track through this

steep-sided glen is wide and well-surfaced. Before Coulshill Farm, a boggy singletrack leads to Cadgers' Yett. This long-established old drove road across the Ochils is also known as Cadgersgait or Tinkers Gate. Cadgers and tinkers were itinerant traders who would visit householders to sell their wares or services.

This part of the route feels very remote. You head up from Coul Burn on a grassy path – which will require pushing at times – to cross the pass (the Cadgers' Yett) and descend into Borland Glen to meet the A823 near Glendevon. Where the formerly tolled road intersects with the Cadgers' Yett lies Glendevon's Tormaukin Hotel, said to have originated as an 18th-century drovers' inn.

The route continues on the road past Castlehill Reservoir to Yetts o' Muckhart, where it overlaps for a short section with the Explore Your Boundaries: Clackmannanshire route. A small road is followed to a house, from where the route uses a combination of tracks to Crook of Devon and its small pub. From the village, you follow a great cycle path for a while over Crook Moss, before joining the B9097 and then another road to Cleish.

From here, Sustrans Route 1 climbs steadily to the top of Dowhill Muir – this road is very popular with road cyclists. To your left are the impressive Nivingston Craigs. From the top, a gravel track leads through Blairadam Forest and underneath the M90 to Keltybridge. The forest offers loads more tracks and is well worth exploring.

From Keltybridge, you follow small roads north to Blairforge, and join the B996 to Blacknowes, tracking the path of the former railway line once again. From here, the B9097 leads to the shore of Loch Leven, where the From Forth to Fife route (page 39) is crossed. If you can lift your bike across two gates, it is possible to access the Loch Leven Heritage Trail at East Brackley. Otherwise, an alternative and easier access point is through the RSPB information centre a bit further down the road – there is an excellent cafe here as well. The multi-user trail is easy to follow counterclockwise around the loch, before the route takes another trail around the golf course and along the High Street past Unorthodox Roasters, another great cafe, back to the start.

08 EXPLORE YOUR BOUNDARIES: CLACKMANNANSHIRE

INTRODUCTION

Explore Your Boundaries, a joint project by the author and cycling-round-the-world record holder Mark Beaumont, was inspired by our desire to create adventures close to home – a way of seeing the familiar in unfamiliar ways. This is one of the 24 routes that explore the boundaries of Scottish councils. One of the most surprising, it offers a great mix of exposed and rugged cycling in the hills combined with scenic and sheltered low-lying paths, circumnavigating the 'Wee County'.

THE ROUTE

The route starts at Alloa railway station and first follows the Alloa Waggonway/Sustrans Route 767, and then a number of roads to the Firth of Forth foreshore. Continue along the Forth to Cambus, where Sustrans Route 76 is joined for a section, passing a number of bonded whisky warehouses. A quiet road takes you from Manor Powis to the A91 Hillfoots Road, with stunning views to the Ochil Hills. Continuing on the A91 into Menstrie, the route soon joins a cycle path and quiet residential roads to the start of the first proper climb.

The small town of Menstrie stands on the floodplain of the River Devon and extends across the Ochil Fault, whose movement gave rise to the dramatic southern scarp of the Ochils. Two of the most westerly summits of the Ochil Hills, Dumyat and Myreton Hill, rise steeply to the north of the town to reach about 400 metres altitude, divided by Menstrie Glen. The hills, combined with nearby Stirling's location at the lowest bridging-point on the River Forth, led to the area's importance as a main gateway to the Highlands. In the early Industrial Revolution, several mill towns such as Tillicoultry, Alva and

ROUTE CONDITIONS

· Singletrack: 27%
· Path: 25%
· Cycle path: 8%
· Road: 40%
· Recommended bike: gravel or mountain bike

The author on the Menstrie switchbacks © Mark Beaumont.

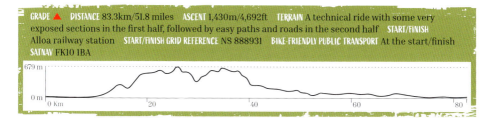

GRADE ▲ DISTANCE 83.3km/51.8 miles ASCENT 1,430m/4,692ft TERRAIN A technical ride with some very exposed sections in the first half, followed by easy paths and roads in the second half START/FINISH Alloa railway station START/FINISH GRID REFERENCE NS 888931 BIKE-FRIENDLY PUBLIC TRANSPORT At the start/finish SATNAV FK10 1BA

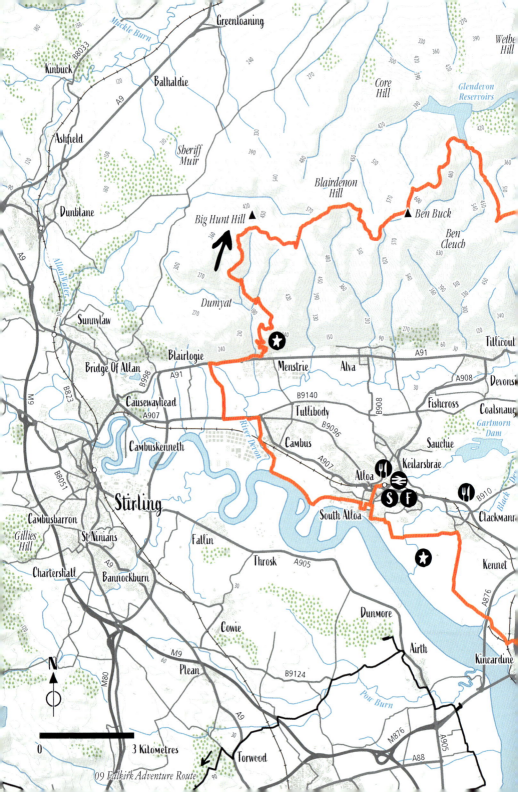

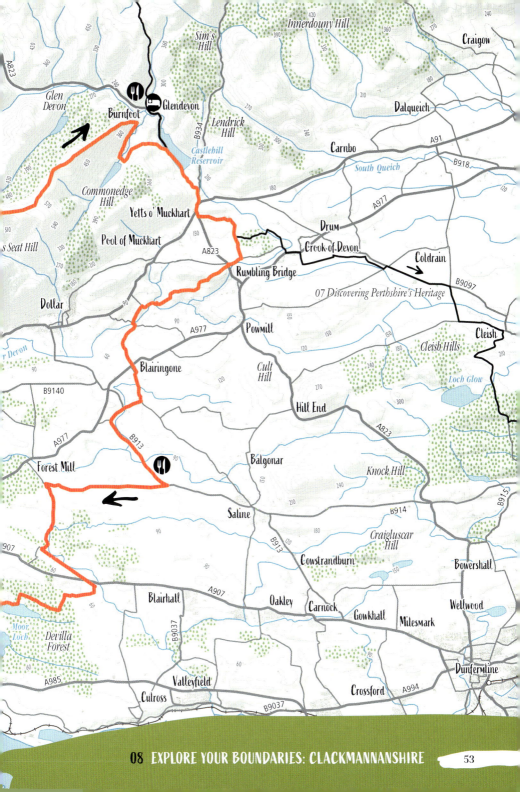

L–R: A lane near Rumbling Bridge; Mark Beaumont traversing the Ochil Hills; Burnfoot Hill wind farm.

Menstrie grew in the shadow of the Ochils to tap the hills' water power. As the mining and textile industries have vanished completely, the surviving old mill buildings have been mostly turned into housing and these towns have transitioned into commuter towns.

Leaving Menstrie, the route climbs very steeply on conspicuous zigzag gravel roadway up the scarp face of Myreton Hill. Nowadays used by the local sheep farmer for access to his livestock, this roadway was originally built to access some calcite mine workings which date from the Napoleonic Wars. This is where the route overlaps with the Clacks gravel route in *Great British Gravel Rides*. This track is perfect for testing your climbing skills and provides fantastic views south over the Forth Valley.

Below Big Hunt Hill, the route climbs further over open moorland and reaches its highest point at 679 metres at Ben Buck. While the riding on this stretch can be tough, especially in wet conditions, the views can make up for the hard work. From the top of the hill, descend towards a big wind farm, where the route joins a wide gravel track. Another descent, this time to Upper Glendevon Reservoir, is one of the best on this route, and there are good opportunities for wild camping here.

After crossing a burn at Backhills, the route climbs steeply back into the Ochil Hills – some sections requiring pushing. The route continues to climb through a steep-sided glen and skirts around Skythorn Hill. Undulating across a number of hills, the route soon descends from Innerdownie into Glen Devon on a singletrack trail. Caution: the last section before reaching Burnfoot is very steep. Here the route connects

with the Discovering Perthshire's Heritage route (page 45). From here, the Cadgers' Yett, an old drove road, is followed to Glenquey Reservoir. A private road leads from here to Castlehill Reservoir, and on to the A823 to Yetts o' Muckhart. This is where the lower section of this route begins.

The route continues on a small road and gravel track to Lendrick Muir, and further towards Rumbling Bridge. Crossing the A823 again, the route continues along the River Devon on gravel tracks to Muckart Mill, and along quiet roads to Vicar's Bridge, and further to Blairingone. After Crow Wood, the route joins the B913 to Saline Shaw Farm, where a cafe and farm shop invite you to stop.

From here, the route follows a small road to Gartgreenie, with great views towards the Ochils. After Brucefield, you join Sustrans Route 764 for around 1.5 kilometres on the track bed of a disused railway line from Dunfermline to Alloa. Near Bogside, you leave the cycle path and continue on gravel paths into Devilla Forest. A singletrack is followed to Peppermill Dam and continues along the northern shore. This section can get muddy. Continue on another nice gravel track to the Scottish Police College at Tulliallan Cottage, and, after crossing the A977, on Sustrans Route 76 to Clackmannan. Leaving the Sustrans route, cross the RSPB Black Devon Wetlands nature reserve on a nice gravel track, before returning on the Alloa Waggonway/ Sustrans Route 767 to Alloa railway station.

FOOD AND DRINK

· The Ladybird Tearoom, Alloa.
  T: 01259 210 102
· Saline Shaw Farm Shop & Cafe, Saline
  – www.salineshawfarmshop.co.uk
· The County Bar, Clackmannan.
  T: 01259 213 462

ACCOMMODATION

· The Tormaukin, Glendevon –
  www.thetormaukin.co.uk

OTHER ROUTES NEARBY

· Discovering Perthshire's Heritage
  (page 45).
· Clacks gravel –
  www.adventurebooks.com/gbgr
· Sustrans National Cycle Network
  routes 76, 767 and 764 –
  www.sustrans.org.uk

BIKE SHOPS AND HIRE

· Alloa Cycle Repairs, Alloa (service).
  T: 01259 222 747

VIDEO INSPIRATION

09 FALKIRK ADVENTURE ROUTE

INTRODUCTION

Falkirk sits right in the heart of Scotland's Central Belt, well-connected to the east and west by trains, and offering adventurous yet very accessible bikepacking routes. Inspired by Roman heritage, architectural wonders and the world-famous Kelpies, this route will help you explore a part of Scotland which is often overlooked.

THE ROUTE

The adventure begins from Falkirk Grahamston railway station on the Edinburgh to Stirling line. As this route also passes Falkirk High station, with more frequent trains on the Edinburgh to Glasgow line, this station can act as an alternative starting point. The route follows the A803 to a roundabout to meet the HArTT (Helix Around Town Tour) route at the Forth and Clyde Canal. You follow the well-graded path along the canal to the Falkirk Wheel, where the route joins Sustrans Route 754 past this rotating boat lift which connects the Forth and Clyde Canal with the Union Canal. Opened in 2002 as part of the Millennium Link project, the Falkirk Wheel is the only rotating boat lift of its kind in the world.

The route climbs shortly and passes through the Roughcastle Tunnel, and soon afterwards crosses the Union Canal to join the John Muir Way into Canada Wood. This and the nearby Tamfourhill Wood offer excellent mountain bike trails which can be used to extend the route if you have time. The route passes a great cafe and bike shop and continues on more nice trails to meet the B803. After a short section on tarmac, the route continues on the JMW to Glen Village, where it rejoins Sustrans Route 754; the first part is a lovely section along the canal through dense woodland, followed by a long section on

ROUTE CONDITIONS

- Singletrack: 4%
- Path: 10%
- Cycle path: 44%
- Road: 42%
- Recommended bike: gravel bike

Louise Chavarie at Roughcastle Tunnel near the Falkirk Wheel.

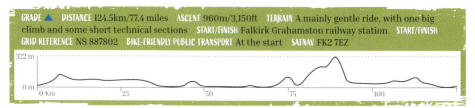

GRADE ▲ DISTANCE 124.5km/77.4 miles ASCENT 960m/3,150ft TERRAIN A mainly gentle ride, with one big climb and some short technical sections START/FINISH Falkirk Grahamston railway station START/FINISH GRID REFERENCE NS 887802 BIKE-FRIENDLY PUBLIC TRANSPORT At the start SATNAV FK2 7EZ

322 m

0 m

0 Km   25   50   75   100

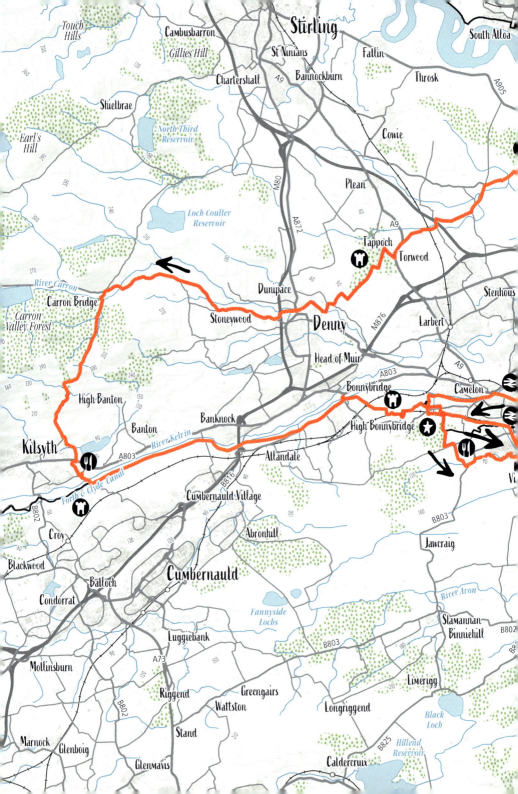

This route is good to ride all year round.

Take care when descending on the Tak-Ma-Doon Road: there are potholes, and it has loose gravel in the bends.

FOOD AND DRINK

- Cafe@Canada Wood, Falkirk.
  T: 01324 612 111
- Steading Cafe, Muiravonside Country Park. T: 01506 845 311
- Taste, Linlithgow. T: 01506 844 445
- Mannerstons Cafe & Farm Shop, near Linlithgow. T: 01506 834 949
- The Lobster Pot, Blackness.
  T: 01506 830 086
- The Corbie Inn, Bo'ness.
  T: 01506 825 307
- The Boathouse Hotel Bar & Restaurant, Auchinstarry.
  T: 01236 829 859

ACCOMMODATION

- West Port Hotel, Linlithgow.
  T: 01506 847 456
- Richmond Park Hotel, Bo'ness.
  T: 01506 823 213

OTHER ROUTES NEARBY

- John Muir Way Bikepacking Route (page 63).
- HArTT route – www.visitfalkirk.com
- Sustrans National Cycle Network routes 76 and 754 – www.sustrans.org.uk
- Explore Your Boundaries: Falkirk – www.bikepackingscotland.com

BIKE SHOPS AND HIRE

- Greenrig Cycles, Falkirk (shop, hire).
  T: 01324 639 619
- Elevation Cycles, Linlithgow (shop).
  T: 01506 845 390

L–R: *The Kelpies; Blackness Castle; Tak-Ma-Doon Road.*

this flat and normally quiet towpath which makes for great and relaxed riding all the way to Muiravonside Country Park. Here, the route loops through the country park and past the small cafe, before rejoining the towpath where you left it and continuing along the Union Canal, again on a long and cruisy section.

Shortly afterwards you pass the Avon Aqueduct, the longest and tallest aqueduct in Scotland. You must push your bike across the structure, but in return you get great views over the River Avon. Continue on the towpath alongside the canal through Linlithgow, where Linlithgow Palace is only a short detour away. In the 15th and 16th centuries, the palace, now mostly a ruin, was one of the principal residences of the monarchs of Scotland. Mary, Queen of Scots was born at Linlithgow Palace in December 1542 and lived here for a while. Linlithgow has plenty of shops, restaurants and cafes, and also offers good choices for accommodation.

You finally leave the canal in the village of Philpstoun, following minor roads north to cross the A904 at Mannerstons – a good stop for lunch or coffee. The next section is first on a private road, and then follows The Strip, a path through a beautiful woodland. The route continues into Blackness, where an excellent pub and Blackness Castle are great options for a stop. Because of its site and long, narrow shape, Blackness Castle has been called 'the ship that never sailed'. It can be visited all year round, and the views from here over the Firth of Forth towards the Forth Bridges are great.

The route continues along the JMW and Sustrans Route 76 along the Firth of Forth to Bo'ness: again, good options for eating and sleeping. The next section of the route follows the Explore Your Boundaries: Falkirk route, which is part of a whole network of routes mapped by Bikepacking Scotland which follow the boundaries of Scottish councils.

The Bo'ness and Kinneil Railway is worth a stop, and after crossing the nearby nature reserve the route continues through the grounds of Kinneil House, passing the remains of the cottage where James Watt worked on developing and improving the steam engine. Continuing along Sustrans Route 76 through the grounds of Kinneil Estate, you can make a short detour to a fun pumptrack in the woods. The remains of the Antonine Wall, built by the Romans between the Firth of Forth and the Firth of Clyde, are clearly visible here.

Follow Sustrans Route 76 all the way through Grangemouth to Auld Toon, where a path along the mouth of the River Carron provides a shortcut to rejoin the signposted Sustrans route at the bridge over the river. A short detour takes you to the Kelpies, Falkirk's biggest tourist attraction. These 30-metre-high horse-

head sculptures can be found alongside a recent extension to the Forth and Clyde Canal. The route continues on mainly quiet roads along the foreshore, and leaves Sustrans Route 76 at Airth. You soon reach The Pineapple, a bizarre fruit-inspired building set within woodland at Dunmore, before continuing on the B9124 and a few country lanes to Torwood, where you are back on gravel through another great woodland. Hidden away in the woods are the Tappoch Broch, an Iron Age broch, and the Torwood Blue Pool, a man-made brick pool of unknown purpose. The route continues on singletracks and gravel tracks into Denny.

From Denny, you first follow a track along the River Carron and then the B818, climbing steadily uphill towards Carron Bridge, from where the famous Tak-Ma-Doon Road crosses the Kilsyth Hills. The route reaches its highest point here at 322 metres, and there are great views over the city of Glasgow. A long-and-fun downhill follows, before the route leaves the road after the quarry and continues on paths through the Colzium Lennox Estate, passing Colzium House.

In Kilsyth, you cross the A803 and continue on an old coach road through woodland to meet the Forth and Clyde Canal. If Roman hillforts are your thing, then a detour to Bar Hill is recommended, although cycling is not permitted on the hillfort. The canal path (JMW) is followed east all the way to Bonnybridge. Using the Radical Pend – a tunnel-like passageway – the route passes underneath the canal and follows the JMW again to Rough Castle fort, another site on the Antonine Wall. Again, cycling is not permitted on this ancient monument. The route then follows tracks through a beautiful woodland to Tamfourhill, passing the Falkirk Wheel for a second time, before continuing along the Union Canal towpath to Glen Village.

Here, the HArTT route is followed into and through Callendar Park on well-surfaced and wide gravel tracks, passing the impressive Callendar House en route. Be mindful that the park can be busy with walkers, families and other users. At the eastern end of the park, you leave the HArTT route to continue on a number of roads to Westquarter and past the Falkirk Distillery. At a motel, the route rejoins the HArTT route to Westfield and finishes back at the railway station.

10 JOHN MUIR WAY BIKEPACKING ROUTE

INTRODUCTION

One of Scotland's Great Trails, the John Muir Way offers a unique coast-to-coast bikepacking journey through Scotland's landscapes, history and heritage, linking Helensburgh in the west with Dunbar, the birthplace of John Muir, in the east. The John Muir Way Bikepacking Route is a combination of the signposted walking and cycling routes, and symbolically passes through Scotland's first national park, Loch Lomond & The Trossachs. This route offers a journey of contrasts and the chance to connect with nature, taking advantage of the green spaces that link the coasts, villages, towns and even the capital city, Edinburgh.

THE ROUTE

Your journey starts at the waterfront in Helensburgh at the John Muir memorial where you'll find a white stone bench and a circular plinth engraved with footprints and a John Muir quote. The town is also the start and finish for the Wild About Argyll Trail (page 81) and is well connected by regular trains to Glasgow and Edinburgh. The Hill House (£), by world-famous Scottish architect Charles Rennie Mackintosh, is passed early on the route and is well worth a visit. The route leaves town on a cycle path alongside Luss Road, before it climbs on a well-maintained gravel road towards Gouk Hill. The views across Loch Lomond & The Trossachs National Park from the top of the hill – a short detour – are awesome. The route continues via a technical singletrack on Stoneymollan Road through the forest. This soon turns into a tarmac road which descends into Balloch.

ROUTE CONDITIONS
· Singletrack: 16%
· Path: 18%
· Cycle path: 41%
· Road: 25%
· Recommended bike: gravel bike

Louise Chavarie on a path at Harestanes Wood near Aberlady.

GRADE ▲ **DISTANCE** 213.2km/132.5 miles **ASCENT** 1,870m/6,135ft **TERRAIN** A great introduction to bikepacking, with only a few technical and remote sections **START/FINISH** John Muir memorial, Helensburgh/John Muir Birthplace Museum, Dunbar **START/FINISH GRID REFERENCE** NS 294822/NT 679789 **BIKE-FRIENDLY PUBLIC TRANSPORT** At Helensburgh Central/Upper and Dunbar railway stations, close to the start/finish **SATNAV** G84 8SQ/EH42 1JJ

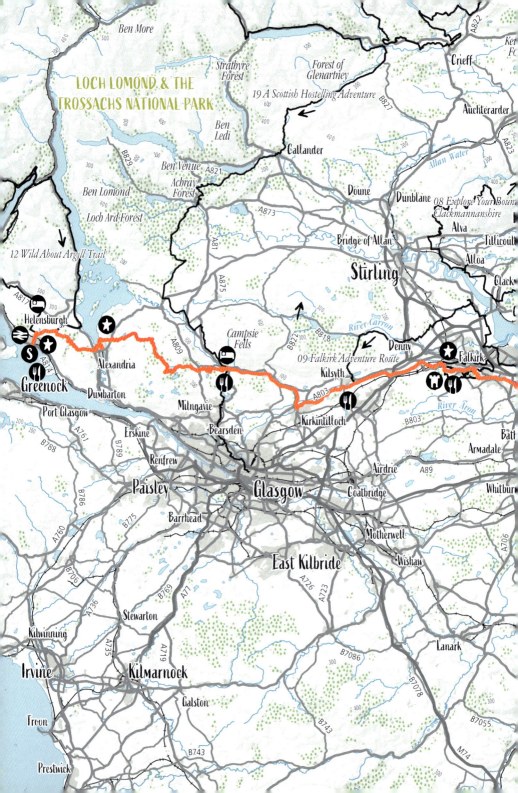

BIKEPACKING SCOTLAND

In Balloch, the route follows minor roads and mixed-use paths along the shores of Loch Lomond. You pass the *Maid of the Loch*, the last and largest in a long line of paddle steamers to sail on Loch Lomond; it is currently undergoing restoration. The route then crosses the River Leven at Balloch railway station, where it connects with Sustrans Route 7 initially but leaves the Sustrans route soon after to follow the riverbank into Balloch Castle Country Park. After the park, the route rejoins Sustrans Route 7 and gradually climbs into the Kilpatrick Hills on minor roads. After crossing the Cameron Burn, the tarmac turns into gravel on the climb towards Burncrooks Reservoir. This section of the route feels very remote. The track along the western and southern shores of Burncrooks Reservoir is fantastic for more experienced off-road riders; if you want an easier ride, the track along the northern shore is a shorter and flatter alternative. After Burncrooks Reservoir, a wider gravel track soon turns into tarmac and passes Edenmill Farm.

Shortly after, the route follows a brief section of Stockiemuir Road, and then crosses Carbeth Hill on a mixture of gravel tracks and paths – overlapping with the West Highland Way for a short section – before descending on Gowk Stane Road into the small town of Strathblane. From here, you follow the Strathkelvin Railway Path (Sustrans Route 755) along the route of several dismantled railway lines as far as Kirkintilloch, passing through Lennoxtown and Milton of Campsie along the way. This smooth and traffic-free cycle path offers great views towards the Campsie Fells to the north, and Dunglass, an ancient volcanic plug, to the south. In Kirkintilloch, the route joins the towpath along the Forth & Clyde Canal, Sustrans Route 754, passing Twechar and the hillfort at Bar Hill. This fort is a remnant of the Antonine Wall, a turf fortification built by the Romans across the Central Belt of Scotland. Auchinstarry Marina provides the opportunity to leave the bike and walk up either Croy Hill or Bar Hill to explore the Roman heritage hereabouts. As these are historical monuments, cycling is not permitted.

Overlapping here with the Falkirk Adventure Route (page 57), your route continues on the towpath to Bonnybridge, where it passes underneath the canal through the Radical Pend.

NAVIGATION

Be mindful that the route described is a mixture of the walking and cycling routes, so don't rely on the signposting.

WHEN TO RIDE

This route is good to ride all year round.

WARNINGS

The technical singletrack on Stoneymollan Road requires pushing down steep steps. While the last third on the East Lothian coast is mainly flat, headwinds can make this a slog.

L–R: Avon Aqueduct on the Union Canal; travel writer Simon Parker crossing a field near North Berwick; John Muir's Birthplace in Dunbar; Yellowcraig Beach with North Berwick in the background.

FOOD AND DRINK

- Sugar Boat, Helensburgh.
  T: 01436 647 522
- Edenmill Cafe and Farm Shop,
  Blanefield. T: 01360 771 707
- The Kirkhouse Inn, Strathblane.
  T: 01360 771 771
- The Boathouse Hotel Bar &
  Restaurant, Auchinstarry.
  T: 01236 829 859
- Cafe@Canada Wood, Falkirk.
  T: 01324 612 111
- Taste, Linlithgow. T: 01506 844 445
- Corbie Inn, Bo'ness. T: 01506 825 307
- The Lobster Pot, Blackness.
  T: 01506 830 086
- Honey Pot Creative Cafe,
  South Queensferry –
  www.honeypotcreativecafe.com
- Harbour Cafe Fisherrow, Musselburgh.
  T: 01968 620 563
- Steampunk Coffee Roasters,
  North Berwick. T: 01620 893 030
- Hector's Artisan Pizzeria, Dunbar –
  www.hectorsdunbar.co.uk

*L–R: Murals in Prestonpans © Gavin
Morton; Gouk Hill near Helensburgh
with Loch Lomond in the background
© Gavin Morton.*

For many years, the pend, a tunnel-like passageway under a structure for pedestrians and cars, was the only way to get from High Bonnybridge to 'low' Bonnybridge, until the bridge was built over the canal. If you are brave, you can cycle through the water that runs through the pend, otherwise a small path on the side will keep your feet dry. The route joins Bonnyside Road and passes Rough Castle, another Roman fort which must be explored on foot (no cycling!). After crossing the railway twice, a path leads to the Falkirk Wheel, one of two working boat lifts in the United Kingdom and the only one of its kind in the world. Boat tours (£) of the wheel and the Union Canal offer a nice distraction from cycling.

After the Falkirk Wheel, a short section through woodland offers a welcome change to the easy towpath cycling, before the route crosses the Union Canal on gravel tracks into Callendar Park. This is a popular mountain bike area and offers a network of trails to explore. The route passes the free-to-access Callendar House, a stunning 14th-century, French-chateau-style house. Climbing through the park, the route meets New Hallglen Road and then follows a path towards the Union Canal, from where it continues on a well-maintained towpath once again. You will need to push your bike over the impressive Avon Aqueduct; carried on 12 arches, it is the tallest and longest aqueduct in Scotland, and the second longest in Britain.

Shortly after the aqueduct, the route leaves the Union Canal and follows the banks of the River Avon into Linlithgow Bridge. Linlithgow Palace (£), one of the principal residences of the monarchs of Scotland in the 15th and 16th centuries, is a short detour. After a section on the road, the route follows paths

and forest tracks. Fishers' Brae, a path once used by wives of fishermen travelling between Bo'ness and Linlithgow to sell their catches, provides superb views. At Kinneil, the public park surrounding the impressive Kinneil House incorporates a section of the Antonine Wall and the only visible example of an Antonine fortlet available today. The route passes the ruins of a small cottage, which was where James Watt devised his improved steam engine in 1765.

After crossing the steam railway tracks, the route follows the Bo'ness foreshore towards Blackness Castle (£). Built in the 15th century and used in various film sets, this is one of Scotland's most picturesque castles. From here, the route follows a well-graded path through the Hopetoun Estate, passing Hopetoun House (£), before joining the shore road into South Queensferry. The From Forth to Fife route (page 39) is met here in the small town. All along this section of the route, the views towards the three bridges over the Firth of Forth are fantastic. The route crosses underneath the Forth Bridge, a UNESCO World Heritage Site, and follows the shore on gravel paths and singletrack sections past Hound Point. After the Dalmeny Estate, it leaves the shore towards Cramond and heads into Scotland's capital city, Edinburgh.

The John Muir Way crosses Corstorphine Hill on singletracks and wider paths before winding its way through town on a mixture of paths along the Water of Leith. After a few steps (with a rail to push bikes up), the route joins the Union Canal towpath for one last time to its terminus at Fountainbridge. The route then passes Arthur's Seat and the distinctively shaped Salisbury Crags in Holyrood Park. From here, a cycle path

ACCOMMODATION
- Travelodge Helensburgh Seafront, Helensburgh. T: 0871 559 1823
- The Attic at Edenmill Farm, Blanefield. T: 01360 770 500
- West Port Hotel, Linlithgow (short detour). T: 01506 847 456
- Richmond Park Hotel, Bo'ness (short detour). T: 01506 823 213
- Orocco Pier Hotel, South Queensferry. T: 0131 331 1298
- Ducks Inn, Aberlady. T: 01875 870 682
- Gilsland Park, North Berwick. T: 01620 893 790
- The Dolphin Inn, Dunbar. T: 01368 868 477

OTHER ROUTES NEARBY
- Go East Lothian Trail (page 25), Capital Trail (page 31), From Forth to Fife (page 39), Falkirk Adventure Route (page 57) and Wild About Argyll Trail (page 91).
- West Highland Way – www.westhighlandway.org
- Sustrans National Cycle Network routes 7, 754 and 755 – www.sustrans.org.uk

BIKE SHOPS AND HIRE

- Helensburgh Cycles (shop, hire).
  T: 01436 675 239
- Greenrig Cycles, Falkirk (shop, hire).
  T: 01324 639 619
- Elevation Cycles, Linlithgow (shop).
  T: 01506 845 390
- Biketrax Edinburgh (shop, hire).
  T: 0131 228 6633
- Ace Bike Co, Musselburgh (shop).
  T: 0131 665 4468
- Law Cycles, North Berwick (shop, hire).
  T: 01620 890 643
- Ez-Riders, North Berwick (hire).
  T: 07407 039 747
- Bethaven Bikes, Dunbar (shop, hire).
  T: 01368 860 300

VIDEO INSPIRATION

L–R: In a beautiful woodland at Tamfourhill near the Falkirk Wheel © Gavin Morton; Blackness Castle with the Queensferry Crossing in the background.

follows the route of the Innocent Railway to Brunstane railway station, where you must push your bike over a bridge. The route continues along Brunstane Burn Path and a short section of main road before reaching Fisherrow Harbour in Musselburgh, where it meets the Capital Trail (page 31).

From here to the finish in Dunbar presents a wealth of wildlife-watching opportunities on the East Lothian coastline. It is also mainly flat, but can be exposed to strong winds. The JMW follows the shore to Morrison's Haven, from where Prestongrange Museum is only a short detour. For centuries, Prestonpans was a place of intense industrial activity: a harbour, glassworks, pottery, colliery and brickworks have all left their marks on the landscape, while today Prestonpans is renowned for its murals. At low tide, the path along the coast is a great experience, but care is needed on the wet and mossy sections. The route passes a large John Muir mural at The Goth pub, and then continues along the shore towards the site of a former power station. At high tide, the road is the best alternative through Prestonpans, rejoining the route shortly after the supermarket at the end of the village.

Continue through Cockenzie and Port Seton and join the road for the next section to Gosford Sands. For wider tyres, the small coastal path is a good alternative to the busy road, but it is lined by hawthorn bushes, whose thorns can cause frequent punctures. Just as the road leaves the shore, a small track on the left leads through a stunning forest, the route lined with

concrete tank barriers built during World War II. Continue through the idyllic village of Aberlady to Aberlady Bay, home to a wealth of wildlife. A great gravel trail leads past a golf course to Gullane, and the route continues through the Archerfield Estate to Dirleton. You then follow a gravel track through fields to Yellowcraig Beach and continue along sandy singletracks and quiet roads into North Berwick.

As the path parallel to the road gets very busy in summer, the B1346 is followed instead. The Scottish Seabird Centre in North Berwick is the start of the Go East Lothian Trail (page 25) and offers tours (£) to Bass Rock in summer. The steep-sided volcanic rock, visible from far afield, is home to a large colony of gannets and puffins. The route passes through the bustling seaside town and past North Berwick Law, a volcano plug that offers great views from the top. With a bit of luck, the resident Exmoor ponies can be spotted on the way to the top, but walking is the much better option here. At the end of the parking lot at North Berwick Law a gap through a wall provides access, but it is difficult to negotiate with a bike; taking the

B1347 Haddington Road for a short section and then rejoining the route by the first minor road on the left is an alternative. The next section of trail through Craigmoor Wood is one of the highlights of the route, before it descends on a mixture of paths into East Linton.

From here, the route passes Preston Mill and continues along the River Tyne, then follows the road for a short while. Passing another set of tank barriers at Tyne Sands, the route reaches John Muir Country Park and continues past Belhaven Bay and along a final – and very scenic – section into Dunbar. The route leaves the JMW at Bayswell Park to avoid several steep sets of steps, and follows Bayswell Road into town, to finish at John Muir's Birthplace on the High Street. Dunbar railway station is close, served by the East Coast Main Line between London King's Cross and Edinburgh. Advance reservations for bikes are needed when taking a bike on the train. Alternatively, the Go East Lothian Trail offers a route back along the coast to North Berwick, from where frequent trains depart to Edinburgh and bike reservations are not mandatory.

ARGYLL & THE ISLES

11 DUNOON DIRT DASH

INTRODUCTION

This route, first used for the annual Dunoon Dirt Dash gravel bikepacking event in 2022, loops the stunning Cowal peninsula. A perfect weekend adventure on the outskirts of Scotland's biggest city, Glasgow, it is the ideal way to experience the rugged beauty of Scotland's Adventure Coast and offers fine gravel riding, majestic woodlands, good food and – of course! – castles.

THE ROUTE

The Dirt Dash starts at the passenger terminal in Dunoon; there are frequent and direct ferry connections from Gourock. You follow the Esplanade and Argyll Street through town, before joining a number of smaller roads to a gravel track climbing steeply into woodland from the western edge of town; you'll get great views from here. Continue on gravel tracks to Glen Kin. As this is an active logging area, there might be some route diversions on this and other sections of the route.

At the bottom of Glen Kin, the route crosses a small burn and continues on Sustrans Route 75. This is the second test for your legs as the route climbs steadily up Glen Lean to Clachaig where the road narrows into a singletrack road. After about four kilometres, a gravel track zigzags steeply up on the right, reaching its highest point above Loch Tarsan. From here, you can enjoy a fast downhill into Glen Tarsan, entering the Loch Lomond & the Trossachs National Park, one of only two national parks in Scotland. After crossing the River Massan, the route heads south-east into Glen Massan on a wide gravel track. This section is home to a resident herd of Highland cattle, so be prepared to make a few detours. From Stonefield, continue on tarmac through a beautiful woodland to Benmore Botanic Garden.

ROUTE CONDITIONS

- Singletrack: 3%
- Path: 60%
- Cycle path: 1%
- Road: 36%
- Recommended bike: gravel or mountain bike

Previous page: Gravel track from Inver Cottage to Feolin Ferry on the Isle of Jura (route 13).

Craig Machine cycling near Lettermay at the annual Dunoon Dirt Dash bikepacking event.

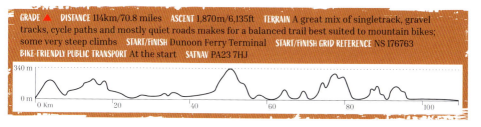

GRADE ▲ **DISTANCE** 114km/70.8 miles **ASCENT** 1,870m/6,135ft **TERRAIN** A great mix of singletrack, gravel tracks, cycle paths and mostly quiet roads makes for a balanced trail best suited to mountain bikes; some very steep climbs **START/FINISH** Dunoon Ferry Terminal **START/FINISH GRID REFERENCE** NS 176763 **BIKE-FRIENDLY PUBLIC TRANSPORT** At the start **SATNAV** PA23 7HJ

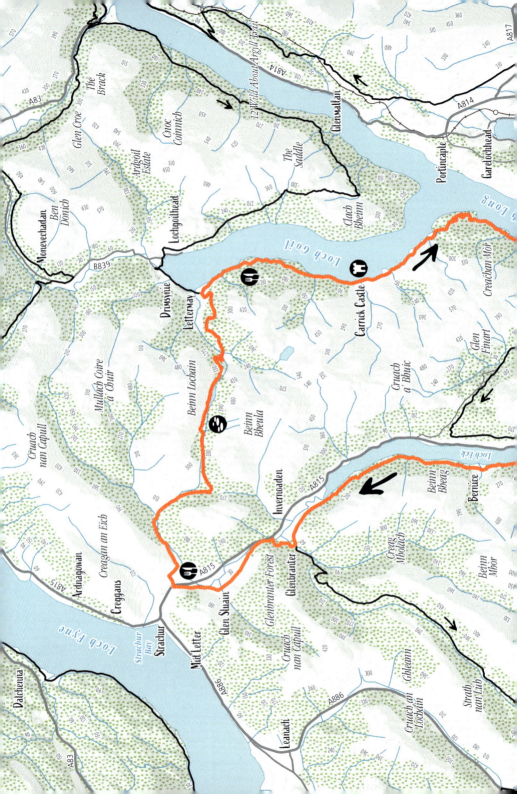

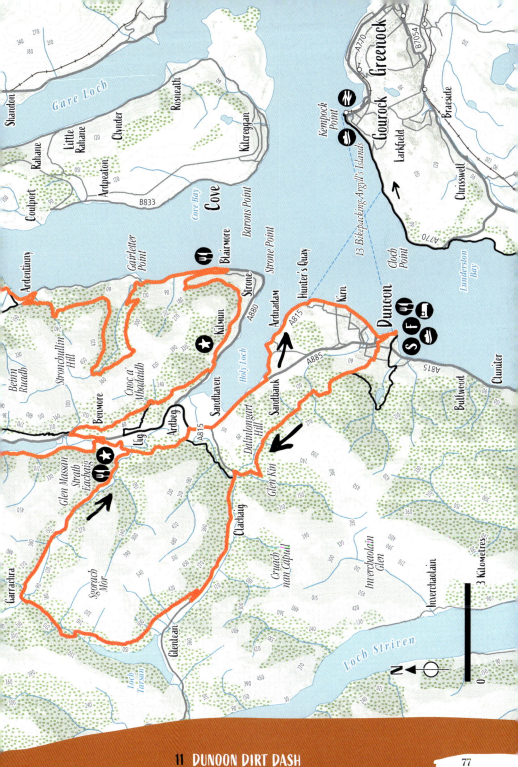

WARNINGS
Be prepared to follow diversions due to logging operations. *Phytophthora ramorum* is a tree disease affecting larch in the area. It can be spread in mud or needles stuck to footwear and tyres on bicycles. Please ensure footwear and bikes are always clean before and after visiting any woodland.

WATER
Note there is a 28-kilometre stretch between Carrick Castle and Blairmore without a water/food stop.

FOOD AND DRINK
· The Lorne, Dunoon. T: 01369 701 777
· Rock Cafe, Dunoon. T: 01369 702 508
· Redwood Coffee at Benmore Botanic Garden, Benmore. T: 01369 706 261
· Strachur Filling Station, Strachur. T: 01369 860 227
· The Boat Shed Café, Loch Goil. T: 01301 707 348
· The Blairmore, Blairmore. T: 01369 760 391

ACCOMMODATION
· Argyll Hotel, Dunoon. T: 01369 702 059
· Carrick Farm B&B, Carrick Castle. T: 01301 703 646

NOTES
For more about the Dunoon Dirt Dash, visit dirtdash.cc
There are two ferry companies serving Dunoon, Calmac (calmac.co.uk) and Western Ferries (www.western-ferries.co.uk). Western Ferries operates a car ferry, which often sails in bad weather conditions when the Calmac service is cancelled.

One of the sites of Royal Botanic Garden Edinburgh, and open daily from 1 March to 31 October, Benmore Botanic Garden (£) is home to a world-famous collection of plants. Its most impressive feature is the Redwood Avenue of giant sequoias, planted in 1863. The route skirts around the garden and then follows the Loch Eck Loop, although in the opposite direction. After passing Benmore Home Farm, you follow a nice wide gravel track that undulates along the western shore of Loch Eck. This 11-kilometre-long loch is one of only two naturally occurring habitats of the powan (Loch Lomond being the other), a freshwater whitefish, as well as salmon, sea trout, brown trout and Arctic charr.

From the northern tip of the loch, you follow a track by the River Cur to Glenshellish Farm and on to Glenbranter, where the route meets the Loch Lomond & Cowal Way, one of Scotland's Great Trails. The route continues on a small road along the River Cur to Strachur, where a small filling station is a great stop for coffee and snacks. From Strachur, the route follows the signposted Loch Lomond & Cowal Way, climbing first on a road, then on a very wide gravel track which turns into a singletrack before Curra Lochain. This section of the route gets gradually tougher, with a river crossing at the beginning and then a rather boggy section along the shores of the loch. Shortly after the loch the route leaves the signposted route and descends steeply on a path to the Lettermay Burn. You continue on a wide gravel track where the signposted route is rejoined, descending all the way to Lettermay on the shore of Loch Goil. From here, the route follows the Wild About Argyll Trail (page 81) on the road to Carrick Castle, passing a nice cafe along the way – this is the last stop for food for about 28 kilometres.

BIKEPACKING SCOTLAND

While Carrick Farm is the location of the campsite for the annual Dunoon Dirt Dash, there is no official campsite here; there is, however, a small B & B (two nights minimum stay). The 15th-century castle is seldom occupied, and the scaffolding has become a permanent feature. Continue on the road, which soon turns into a track and climbs steeply through the forest, before descending on a wider track into Ardentinny. From here, the route follows the Laird's Trail along the shore and, after a short section on the public road, then climbs steeply into another woodland. Be prepared for fallen trees and logging operations along this whole stretch around Ardentinny.

After a short downhill, the route continues into the Blairmore Horseshoe, which offers fine gravel riding and great views on a clear day. The route then descends through the beautiful Gairletter Forest to meet the road just south of Gairletter Point and continues along the shore of Loch Long to Blairmore, which has an excellent cafe. A small street climbs out of the village and turns into singletrack, skirting around Blairmore Hill. The route continues on a gravel track that descends into Kilmun, where the Dukes of Argyll are laid to rest in a mausoleum beside St Munn's Church.

One last steep hill follows, climbing the tarmac road to a car park at the entrance to Kilmun Arboretum, home to more than 150 species of tree from around the world. You continue on a nice wide gravel track, passing Puck's Glen, one of the best walks in Scotland. At Inverchapel, the route joins the A815 back to Benmore. At the gardens, the route crosses the River Eachaig and follows a small track along its banks, before joining a minor road to Invereck. From here, there is a cycle path along the A815 before the route continues on Sustrans Route 75 back to the ferry terminal in Dunoon.

OTHER ROUTES NEARBY
· Wild About Argyll Trail (page 81).
· Explore Your Boundaries: Argyll and the Isles – page 100 and www.bikepackingscotland.com
· Sustrans National Cycle Network Route 75 – www.sustrans.org.uk
· Loch Eck Loop – www.lochlomond-trossachs.org
· Loch Lomond & Cowal Way – www.scotlandsgreattrails.com
· Action Argyll routes – www.actionargyll.com/gravel-cycling

BIKE SHOPS AND BIKE HIRE
· Start Line MTB Dunoon Bike Hire, Dunoon (hire) – www.startlinemtb.com
· Duncan MacLeod Cycling Services, Dunoon (service). T: 07775 652 888
· Woodside Bikeworks, Dunoon (service). T: 07974 198 664

VIDEO INSPIRATION

L–R: *Jenny Graham in a woodland at Ardentinny; riders on gravel paths above Lettermay.*

12 WILD ABOUT ARGYLL TRAIL

INTRODUCTION

Bikepacking Scotland's first long-distance gravel bikepacking trail was published in 2018, and it has since been ridden by many riders seeking an amazing adventure on gravel tracks, forest roads, singletrack, cycle paths and quiet roads. It can be ridden in one go, or split up into different sections which are well-served by public transport. Off the saddle, there's plenty of opportunity to taste whisky and craft beers, to go island-hopping, swim in crystal-clear water, breathe pure air, watch magnificent sunsets and let the dark skies take your breath away.

THE ROUTE

Easily accessible with frequent trains from Edinburgh, Glasgow and Oban, this route starts in Helensburgh, a graceful town with wide, elegant and tree-lined streets, a long promenade, and attractive parks and gardens. It is also home to the Hill House (£), a masterpiece by the Scottish architect Charles Rennie Mackintosh, and is the start (or finish) of the John Muir Way (page 63).

Climbing out of the town, the route follows the Three Lochs Way on the line of an ancient coffin road and drove road, the Highlandman's Road, which takes you into Glen Fruin. Here, the route first follows a small road and then a gravel track to Gleann Culanach, still on the signposted route of the Three Lochs Way. The route leaves the track and continues on a road to the A814 into Arrochar.

Now in Argyll Forest Park, the first forest park to be designated in the UK, the route continues from Arrochar through Succoth, joins the Glen Loin Loop for a short section

ROUTE CONDITIONS

- Singletrack: 4%
- Path: 32%
- Cycle path: 4%
- Road: 59%
- Ferry: 1%
- Recommended bike: gravel bike

The author, Jenny Graham and Mark Beaumont on the east coast of the Kintyre Peninsula © Maciek Tomiczek.

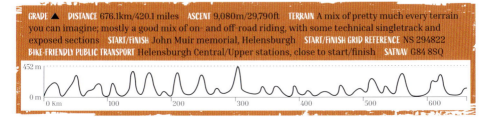

GRADE ▲ **DISTANCE** 676.1km/420.1 miles **ASCENT** 9,080m/29,790ft **TERRAIN** A mix of pretty much every terrain you can imagine; mostly a good mix of on- and off-road riding, with some technical singletrack and exposed sections **START/FINISH** John Muir memorial, Helensburgh **START/FINISH GRID REFERENCE** NS 294822 **BIKE-FRIENDLY PUBLIC TRANSPORT** Helensburgh Central/Upper stations, close to start/finish **SATNAV** G84 8SQ

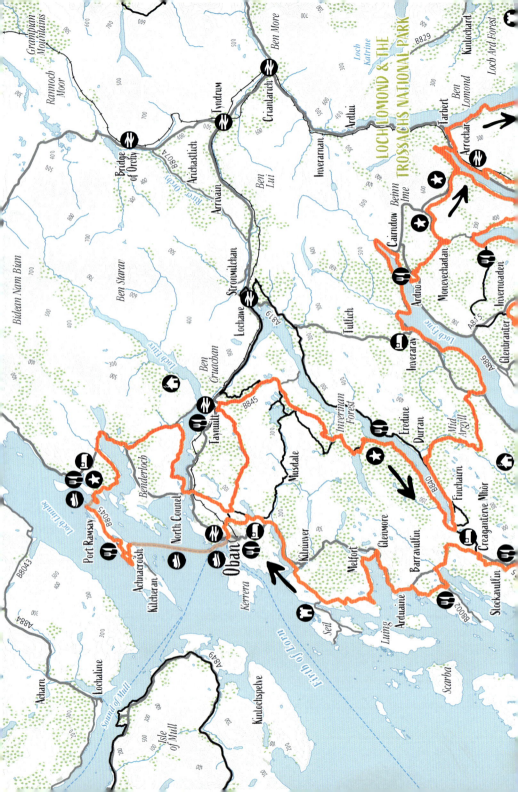

WHEN TO RIDE

This epic route is good all year round.

WARNINGS

The Duke's Path to Lochgoilhead includes a downhill section that might test some riders. The A83 is a busy road, which can't be avoided at times. Take care, especially before and after ferries arrive, as lorries are using the road. The gravel road towards Allt Dearg wind farm and the highest point of the route at 452 metres is very exposed.

NOTES

Saddle Skedaddle offers guided trips on the Wild About Argyll Trail – www.skedaddle.com

L–R: The author and Jenny Graham at the start of the John Muir Way and Wild About Argyll Trail in Helensburgh; Matthias Stitz on the Bridge over the Atlantic; tasty food from the Seafood Hut in Oban.

and continues on a forest road. On the right a walking track climbs up to the Cobbler, also known as Ben Arthur, one of the most recognisable peaks in the Arrochar Alps. The route continues on the forest road, and shortly afterwards on some great singletrack switchbacks to a car park and toilet at Ardgartan. From here, the route follows the Cat Craig Loop first and then continues on the very scenic Ardgartan Peninsula Circuit with views over Loch Long. Mark Cottage, a Mountain Bothies Association (MBA) bothy, is situated off the route on the shore of Loch Long. This section of the route is also part of the Loch Lomond & Cowal Way. After a perfect spot for a stop at Corran Lochan, you can soon enjoy the great views over the hills and Loch Goil from the Duke's Path, including a downhill section that might test some riders.

From Lochgoilhead, the route follows a quiet road for a stretch, overlapping with the Dunoon Dirt Dash route (page 75). Soon after Carrick Castle, the road ends and a track follows the shores of Loch Goil and later joins a good forest track to Ardentinny. The route passes Ardentinny Bay and the longest beach on the Cowal peninsula, and then follows another quiet road for a bit and climbs towards Loch Eck on a gravel road to join the Loch Eck Loop on the eastern side of the loch. The wide track turns into a singletrack and then back into a gravel track, passing near Benmore Botanic Garden with its magnificent Redwood Avenue, before reaching Puck's Glen. This hike-a bike section on a very popular walking route is worth the effort. Puck's Glen is a deep gorge with a tumbling burn, criss-crossed by bridges and enclosed by rocky cliffs, heavily hung with mosses and overshadowed by dense trees. The route continues on the A815 from Uig Hall and joins Sustrans Route 75 into Dunoon, the main town on the beautiful Cowal peninsula

and the maritime gateway to Loch Lomond & The Trossachs National Park. It is served by a passenger ferry from Gourock railway station, which makes for a good alternative start or finish point.

From Dunoon, the route climbs up a gravel track with great views over Holy Loch to cross the B836, and then follows a quiet road along the Little Eachaig River and River Eachaig. After passing Benmore Botanic Garden (£), a gravel track follows the shore of Loch Eck all the way to Glenbranter, where the route rejoins the Loch Lomond & Cowal Way. After a great cycle through the forest, the views which open up towards the west are spectacular, and after a short section on the A886 you follow a quiet road to Clachan of Glendaruel. Shortly afterwards, the route climbs on a forest track heading south, with great views back to the north. After this section on a well-maintained timber logging route, the Wild About Argyll Trail joins the B8000 before Millhouse. From here, it follows Sustrans Route 75 to Kames and then a quiet road loops back to Millhouse, and from there on to Portavadie. This is the first of a few sections where the Wild About Argyll Trail overlaps with Explore Your Boundaries: Argyll and the Isles (page 100). From Portavadie, a ferry with frequent daily services runs across Loch Fyne to the picturesque fishing village of Tarbert.

From the ferry terminal, the route leads through the village and on to the Kintyre Way. Passing Tarbert Castle, the first climb is very steep, but you will be rewarded with a nice forest road and a great downhill to the coast at Skipness. After great views on the quiet road along the coast south from Skipness, the route joins the Caledonia Way in Claonaig. This section on the singletrack road at the eastern side of the Kintyre peninsula makes up for more steep climbs with great views

FOOD AND DRINK
- Sugar Boat, Helensburgh.
  T: 01436 647 522
- Heather & Thyme @ The Boat Shed,
  Lochgoilhead. T: 01301 707 348
- The Blairmore, Blairmore (detour).
  T: 01369 760 391
- The Lorne, Dunoon. T: 01369 701 777
- The Coffee Bar At Hayshed Gallery,
  Tighnabruaich. T: 01700 385 538
- Cafe Ca'Dora, Tarbert.
  T: 01880 820 258
- Kilmartin Hotel, Kilmartin.
  T: 01546 510 250
- Lucy's, Ardfern. T: 01852 500 781
- Seafood Hut (Green Shack), Oban.
  T: 07881 418 565
- Isle of Lismore Cafe, Lismore.
  T: 01631 760 030
- The Pierhouse Hotel, Port Appin.
  T: 01631 730 302
- The Robin's Nest, Taynuilt.
  T: 01866 822 429
- Wild Rowan Cafe, Dalavich.
  T: 01866 844 256

- Riva Boutique Hotel, Helensburgh.
 T: 01436 677 796
- Argyll Hotel, Dunoon.
 T: 01369 702 059
- Starfish Rooms, Tarbert.
 T: 01880 820 324
- Ferry Farm Bed & Breakfast,
 Tayinloan. T: 01583 441 141
- Oban Youth Hostel, Oban.
 T: 01631 562 025
- The Pierhouse Hotel, Port Appin.
 T: 01631 730 302
- Ederline Estate Guest House, Ford.
 T: 01546 810 284
- Crown House Bed and Breakfast, Ford.
 T: 01546 810 279
- Inveraray Hostel, Inveraray.
 T: 01499 302 562

L–R: On the road from Degnish to Melfort; Oban – Scotland's Seafood Capital.

across to Arran. Near Grogport, the Wild About Argyll Trail leaves the tarmac and climbs on a very good gravel track towards the Deucheran Hill wind farm.

In Killean, the route joins the A83 through Tayinloan, with the chance to hop on a ferry to the Isle of Gigha. The section of the A83 can be busy, but a short detour on a quiet side road at Clachan is the perfect opportunity to soak in the views over to Islay and Jura. The route continues on the A83 passing Kennacraig, the main terminal for ferries to the Isle of Islay and onwards to Jura. To cut your trip short, you can take the ferry to Islay and on to Oban on certain days. It is here that the route connects with the Bikepacking Argyll's Islands route (page 91). Continue on the road back to Tarbert.

The section north of Tarbert on the A83 travels along the beautiful shoreline of Loch Fyne, before leaving the road at Stronchullin Burn to climb on a gravel road towards Allt Dearg wind farm and the highest point of the route at 452 metres. The views towards the Firth of Clyde in the east and Loch Caolisport in the west are breathtaking and worth the long climb. After a fast descent, the Caledonia Way is rejoined briefly to Achahoish, and then the very quiet coastal road past St Columba's Cave to Ellary House offers more great views. From here, the private Ellary Road climbs steeply and becomes a track which joins the East Loch Sween Road near Kilmory. The route passes the 13th-century Kilmory Knap Chapel with its medieval sculptures.

The route continues along the shores of Loch Sween past Castle Sween to Achnamara. Shortly afterwards, it leaves the road to follow the Lochan Buic Cycle Trail to the Crinan Canal. The Argyll Beaver Centre is only a short and worthwhile detour from the route. You cross the B841 and then the Crinan Canal at lock 9, and continue along the towpath westbound to Bellanoch.

From here, the route continues on the Caledonia Way north to Kilmartin, passing Dunadd Fort, where ancient kings of Scotland were crowned. Kilmartin Glen is one of Scotland's most significant archaeological landscapes, with unique Neolithic and Bronze Age remains along the route.

Shortly after Carnasserie Castle, the route joins the A816 until Loch Craignish, where the quieter B8002 takes you to Ardfern and a gravel road across the hill to Craobh Haven. After a section on a track along the shores of the Sound of Shuna, the route rejoins the A816 north towards Kilmelford, and continues on a winding singletrack road to the start of the Bealach Gaoithe, the 'pass of the winds'. This is a great remote section from the Degnish Peninsula to Ardmaddy Bay, passing the Wishing Tree in a wooden enclosure along the way. From Ardmaddy, a short detour takes you to the Clachan Bridge, a single-arched, humpback masonry bridge spanning the Clachan Sound. Because the Clachan Sound connects at both ends to the Atlantic Ocean, the bridge became known as the 'Bridge over the Atlantic'. Nearby, the island of Easdale hosts the annual World Stone Skimming Championships each September.

Near Kilninver, the route rejoins the A816 to Kilmore, where a quieter road takes you past the tranquil Loch Nell and over open moorland to Glencruitten Road and on to the ferry terminal in Oban – regular ferries operate to the Inner and Outer Hebrides and the Hebridean Way. Surrounded by miles of dramatic coastline and beautiful countryside, this seaside town is also known as Scotland's Seafood Capital, and is well connected to Glasgow by the Highland Explorer train service. It provides a great alternative start and finish point.

From Oban, a ferry takes you to the island of Lismore, where

OTHER ROUTES NEARBY

· John Muir Way (page 63), Dunoon Dirt Dash (page 75), Bikepacking Argyll's Islands (page 91) and Around Loch Awe (page 103).

· Explore Your Boundaries: Argyll and the Isles – page 100 and www.bikepackingscotland.com

· Three Lochs Way, Loch Lomond & Cowal Way and Kintyre Way – www.scotlandsgreattrails.com

· Sustrans National Route 75 – www.sustrans.org.uk

· Explore Your Boundaries: Argyll and the Isles – www.bikepackingscotland.com

· Caledonia Way (parts are Sustrans Route 78) – www.visitscotland.com

· Hebridean Way – www.visitouterhebrides.co.uk

NOTES

· Ferries on this route: CalMac (www.calmac.co.uk) Portavadie to Tarbert, and Oban to Lismore; and Argyll & Bute Council (www.argyll-bute.gov.uk/port-appin-point-lismore-ferry-timetable) Point (Lismore) to Port Appin.

BIKE SHOPS AND HIRE

- Helensburgh Cycles, Helensburgh
  (shop, hire). T: 01436 675 239
- Campbell Bike Workshop, Arrochar.
  T: 07811 123 943
- Start Line MTB Dunoon Bike Hire,
  Dunoon (hire) – www.startlinemtb.com
- Duncan MacLeod Cycling Services,
  Dunoon (service). T: 07775 652 888
- Woodside Bikeworks, Dunoon (service).
  T: 07974 198 664
- Rusty Cycle Shed, Taynuilt (shop, hire).
  T: 07791 974 152
- Oban Cycles, Oban (shop, hire).
  T: 01631 566 033
- Lismore Bike Hire, Isle of Lismore.
  T: 07376 425 996
- Appin Electric Bikes, Appin.
  T: 07935 229 667

VIDEO INSPIRATION

L–R: *Phone box with the famous
German Gartenzwerg; Mark Beaumont
and Jenny Graham on Lochan Buic
Cycle Trail.*

the route continues from Achnacroish, first on a road and then on a gravel track to a disused lime kiln. The road is rejoined for a short while, and, after another off-road section, the route reaches the northern end of the small island, from where a passenger ferry departs every hour to Port Appin.

From the Pierhouse Hotel, a gravel track takes you to a split rock before the route continues on a singletrack road around the Appin peninsula. If you want to see one of Scotland's most photographed castles, Castle Stalker, which occupies a tiny island to the north of the village, then follow the road in the opposite direction and join the Caledonia Way. The Wild About Argyll Trail otherwise follows the quiet road along the shore of Loch Creran, where otters are often spotted, and then a short, traffic-free section on the Caledonia Way to Barcaldine and Sutherland's Grove, from where the route follows the quiet B845 to the shores of Loch Etive.

Cadderlie Bothy, on the north shore of Loch Etive, is another worthwhile detour and a good overnight stop. The bothy is featured in Scottish songwriter Dougie MacLean's song 'Eternity' and is all that remains of what was once a proper settlement. A quiet road follows the shore of Loch Etive to North Connel, where the route joins the Caledonia Way through the picturesque Glen Lonan to Taynuilt, which is on the Glasgow to Oban railway line.

From Taynuilt, the route follows the B845 through Glen Nant National Nature Reserve. You cycle amongst its lush Atlantic oakwoods, which historically provided the charcoal for the Bonawe Iron Furnace just north of Taynuilt. A service road for a wind farm then takes you into the planted forests above Loch Awe and along gravel 'highways' to Loch Avich. Parts of

the route from here overlap with the Around Loch Awe route (page 103). After a short section along the shore of the loch, the route travels into the River Avich valley, passing the impressive Avich Falls, before Dalavich offers a good opportunity to stop.

At Newyork the route joins the old forest track along the shore of Loch Awe to Kilmaha, before continuing along the Caledonia Way to Ford. From Ford, the quiet B840 follows the eastern shores of Loch Awe to the start of the former Leacainn Forest Drive. This part of the route takes you on a great gravel track through woodland and wild moor to Loch Fyne. For the adventurous, Carron Bothy is about two kilometres off the route: look out for a track on your right before the forest road curves to the south at a clearing. The route joins the A83 for a short section before continuing from Furnace along the shores of Loch Fyne to a caravan site and, after another short stint on the main road, on to Inveraray. This small, planned town is the ancestral home of the Duke of Argyll.

From here the route follows the A83, with a few smaller sections off the road. Cairndow, a coastal hamlet on Loch Fyne, marks the start of a trail that follows the east shore of Loch Fyne and then climbs to join the A815 for a

short while to the Tinkers' Heart, a monument to Scottish Travellers. Climbing on the B839 through Hell's Glen, the Wild About Argyll Trail takes in one of Scotland's iconic road climbs, before joining the Ardgartan Peninsula Circuit almost to the top of the Rest and Be Thankful pass. If you make the detour to the top, there are fantastic views from here across the old valley road which was engineered by General Wade. Travelling away from the busy road on a much quieter gravel track, the route joins a small path from the Ardgartan car park to the shores of Loch Long, and then travels alongside the A83 to Arrochar.

From here, the route follows the Three Lochs Way and joins the A83 into Tarbert on the shores of Loch Lomond. The West Loch Lomond Cycle Path marks one of the last sections of the route, an easy-going journey with spectacular views of Loch Lomond and its famous islands, Conic Hill, and the most southerly Munro, Ben Lomond. The pretty village of Luss is well worth exploring and offers the opportunity for well-earned refreshments. At Arden Roundabout, the route follows the A818 and then the cycle path back into Helensburgh, where it finishes at the John Muir memorial.

13 BIKEPACKING ARGYLL'S ISLANDS

INTRODUCTION

Argyll's islands – the Inner Hebrides and Bute – offer fantastic bikepacking, with beautiful beaches, some of the world's best distilleries, great gravel tracks and local food experiences. In an itinerary which can be started and finished in Glasgow, the host city of the 2023 UCI Cycling World Championships, this route combines public transport with ScotRail's Highland Explorer, relaxing ferry journeys and great cycling on the islands of Mull, Jura, Islay and Bute. For new bikepackers and gravel cyclists, Bikepacking Argyll's Islands offers a wide range of accommodation and incentives to stop, while experienced cyclists will find plenty of opportunities to further extend the route.

THE ROUTE

After taking the train from Glasgow and then the ferry from Oban, you start the route at the ferry terminal in Craignure on the Isle of Mull. Follow the A849 out of the village and, immediately after passing a golf course on the right, a beautiful beach invites you to stop; a standing stone can also be spotted in the field on the opposite side of the road. After Scallastle Bay the route takes a track on the right – this has recently been upgraded in stages and offers fantastic off-road cycling. It passes the Fishnish ferry terminal which has frequent connections to Lochaline on the Morvern peninsula. For those wanting to extend the route, there are a number of additional trails in the forest too.

Shortly afterwards, the route follows a track on the left at Leiter and rejoins the road again near a woodland. The well-graded gravel track is a nice alternative to the road but beware of livestock (cattle) in the fields. The route passes Glenforsa

ROUTE CONDITIONS

· Singletrack: 2%
· Path: 14%
· Cycle path: 10%
· Road: 55%
· Ferry: 19%
· Recommended bike: gravel bike

Philippa Battye and Josh Ibbett on Britain's loneliest A road on the Isle of Jura.

GRADE ▲ **DISTANCE** 611.2km/379.8 miles **ASCENT** 5,180m/16,995ft **TERRAIN** A great touring route, with little technical off-road riding and few exposed sections **START/FINISH** Craignure ferry terminal, Isle of Mull/ Gourock railway station **START/FINISH GRID REFERENCE** NM 717371/NS 242779 **BIKE-FRIENDLY PUBLIC TRANSPORT** At start/finish, with train and ferry links to Glasgow **SATNAV** PA65 6AY/PA19 1QR

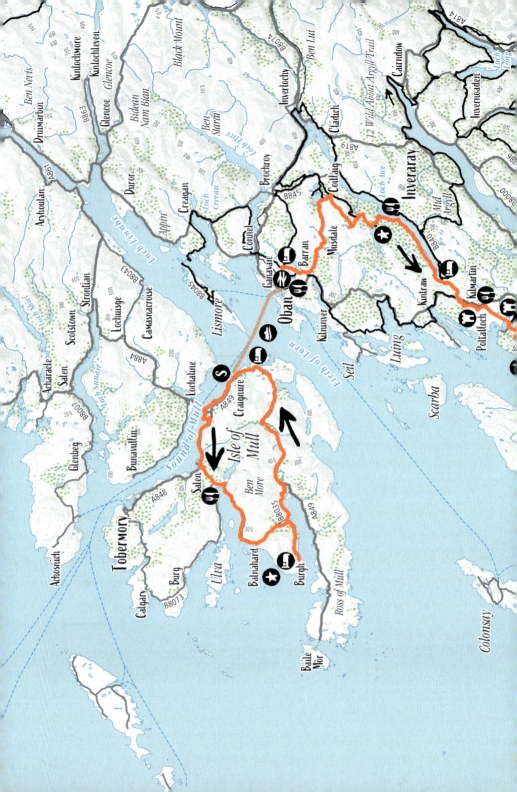

airfield and continues into Salen. A small detour to the old Salen Pier passes a campsite and offers stunning views over Salen Bay.

From Salen, the route continues on the B8035 towards Gruline and then along the shore of Loch na Keal, with outstanding views towards the mountains and the sea. A steep climb takes you away from the coast. Once the highest point is reached, follow a gravel track that branches off to the right down Gleann Seilisteir. From Tiroran, the route follows a farm track into Burg, ending at Burg bothy which is under the ownership of the National Trust for Scotland. Out of reach for bikes, MacCulloch's fossil tree offers a worthwhile excursion on foot. Please check the tide before you set off, as some sections of this coastal walk are only accessible at low tide.

Backtracking to Tiroran, the route continues on a singletrack tarmac road and joins the B8035 along the shore of Loch Scridain and further on to Loch Beg. The views towards the mountains are stunning, and shortly afterwards a short section of gravel track connects the B8035 with the A849 through Glen More. Parts of the old road can be spotted on either side of the new road; some sections are suitable for riding, while others offer you the finest bog you can find in Scotland. Shortly after Torness the route continues on a track on the right, following the Lussa River downstream. This track meets the road at Strathcoil, from where you continue on tarmac to the ferry terminal at Craignure.

After a ride back to Oban the next section starts at the ferry terminal and follows the Caledonia Way out of town before descending towards Loch Nell. The route continues on this road until just before Kilmore, and then on towards Musdale. The road climbs through the valley towards Musdale and then follows a gravel track on the left towards Loch Nant. This remote section offers fantastic off-road riding, before an old asphalt road takes you to the shore of the loch and along its southern edge. Shortly afterwards, the route follows a logging road to the right through a wind farm. This 'gravel highway' provides great views over Loch Awe and the surrounding forests, before the track descends and joins the Kilmelford

WHEN TO RIDE
This route is good to ride all year round.

WARNINGS
The roads on Mull can get busy in peak season, and are best avoided just before and immediately after ferries arrive. Check ferry times and sailings before setting off.

FOOD AND DRINK
- The Coffee Pot, Salen. T: 01680 300 555
- Seafood Hut (Green Shack), Oban. T: 07881 418 565
- Wild Rowan Cafe, Dalavich. T: 01866 844 256
- Kilmartin Hotel, Kilmartin. T: 01546 510 250
- Tayvallich Café, Tayvallich. T: 01546 870 364
- The Antlers Bistro Restaurant, Craighouse. T: 01496 305 317
- Port Askaig Hotel and Stores, Port Askaig. T: 01496 840 245
- Old Kiln Cafe, Ardbeg. T: 01496 302 244
- Cafe Ca'Dora, Tarbert. T: 01880 820 258
- Five West, Tighnabruaich. T: 01700 811 022
- Mount Stuart Restaurant, Mount Stuart. T: 01700 503 877
- Harry Haw's, Rothesay. T: 01700 505 857

L–R: Josh Ibbett at Machir Bay, Islay; a dram at Bunnahabhain Distillery, Islay; deer at Craighouse, Jura; Calmac ferry from Oban to Craignure, Mull.

to Dalavich road. At Dalavich, the route overlaps with the Wild About Argyll Trail (page 81) and Around Loch Awe (page 103). From here, the route follows the road first, before joining a track along the shore at Newyork, which climbs steeply back towards the road. From here the route continues on the Caledonia Way to Ford.

Follow the Caledonia Way to a parking space near the ruin of Carnassarie Castle, north of Kilmartin. This area's history spans 5,000 years, with a multitude of cairns, standing stones, carved rock, stone circles, forts and castles – it is considered to have one of the most important concentrations of Neolithic and Bronze Age remains in Scotland. While the path towards the castle ruin is steep and the ground here can get muddy at times, following this off-road section of the Caledonia Way is worth the effort. After Kilmartin the route continues on the road again across Mòine Mhòr. Depending on the wind direction, this super-straight stretch of road can be challenging or enjoyable in equal measure.

The route leaves the Caledonia Way and follows the road along a short section of the Crinan Canal and then the B8025 to Tayvallich. Here the Jura Passenger Ferry runs to Craighouse on the Isle of Jura between the start of March and the end of September; it must be booked in advance. As an alternative, you can also get to Jura with Venture West, which operates out of Crinan Harbour and drops cyclists off at the northern end of the island. See opposite page for ferry information.

From Craighouse on the Isle of Jura the route continues north through the village on the A846, also known as the Long Road. Expect much less traffic and a few more potholes than on

· Sustrans National Cycle Network
  routes 75 and 753 –
  www.sustrans.org.uk
· Caledonia Way (parts are on Sustrans
  Route 78) – www.visitscotland.com
· Kintyre Way – www.thekintyreway.com

BIKE SHOPS AND HIRE

· Oban Cycles, Oban (shop, hire).
  T: 01631 566 033
· Islay Cycles, Port Ellen (shop, hire).
  T: 07760 196 592
· Kayak Wild Islay, Port Ellen (hire).
  T: 07973 725 456
· The Bike Shed, Rothesay (shop).
  T: 01700 505 515

NOTES

· Ferries on this route:
  Calmac (www.calmac.co.uk)
  Oban to Craignure (Mull),
  Port Askaig (Islay) to Kennacraig,
  Tarbert to Portavadie,
  Colintraive to Rhubodach (Bute), and
  Rothesay (Bute) to Wemyss Bay;
  Jura Passenger Ferry
  (www.jurapassengerferry.com)
  Tayvallich to Craighouse (Jura);
  Venture West (www.venture-west.co.uk)
  Charter service to Jura;
  Argyll & Bute Council
  (www.argyll-bute.gov.uk/port-askaig-
  islay-feolin-jura-ferry-timetable)
  Feolin (Jura) to Port Askaig (Islay).
· Dan the Merman, a professional
  wild swim guide, offers guided
  wild swim/snorkel experiences for
  all abilities along this route.
  www.swimdanthemerman.com

VIDEO INSPIRATION

a usual A-road. The route continues past a beautiful bay to Lagg, where it climbs steeply into a woodland and descends to the narrowest part of the island at Tarbert. You can find a standing stone and the remains of a chapel in the field at Tarbert Bay. A gravel track to the left leads down to Loch Tarbert, where once drovers landed their cattle and transferred them across the track to Tarbert Bay to continue their journey to the mainland.

The route backtracks to Craighouse and continues south on the Long Road around the southern tip of Jura to Feolin Ferry. From here the route follows the Deer Island gravel route from *Great British Gravel Rides*. This loop offers great views towards Islay and the Paps of Jura. The ferry from Feolin runs frequently to Port Askaig on Islay, and timetable and fare information can be found on the Argyll and Bute Council website (see right).

Out of Port Askaig the first 14-per-cent climb on the road will warm you up, before the route takes a small track through a gate on the left which leads to a loch. The track becomes wider here and takes you through a beautiful woodland on a wide track and past another, bigger, loch. Shortly after the loch, the route joins the tarmac again on Glen Road. The route follows Glen Road south, past the wonderfully rugged hills on Islay's eastern coast. While it is tempting to try some of the gravel tracks that leave the road to the left, sooner or later they'll end in a deep bog. The route follows Glen Road and then meets High Road into Port Ellen. From here the route follows the A846 out of town and a cycle path to three distilleries: Laphroaig, Lagavulin and Ardbeg. You could easily spend a day visiting and enjoying the pretty coastline. From Ardbeg, the route returns the same way, passes through Port Ellen and takes a left at the end of the town.

*L–R: Josh Ibbett and Philippa Battye
in a woodland on Jura's west coast.*

A singletrack trail on the left takes you through another beautiful woodland to a beach and then on a wider track back to the road. From here, the route continues on a short section of gravel on the right to connect with the A846 main road to Bowmore. This is flat and enjoyable, but be mindful of passing traffic. An alternative for those with wide tyres and loads of time is riding on the beach of Laggan Bay almost all the way to Bowmore. Past Bowmore the route continues to Bruichladdich on road, and on a final section of segregated cycle path to Port Charlotte.

From Port Charlotte, the route follows School Street west out of town, with a nice climb to warm up the legs. After Kilchiaran Farm on the right a gravel track climbs gently north and descends towards Machir Bay. This is one of the most stunning bays on Islay, so bring time. There is livestock in the fields the track passes and at times a detour is necessary to avoid cows with their calves.

After Machir Bay the route joins a small tarmac road to loop around Loch Gorm before returning to the coast. Shortly after Ballygrant, the route follows a small road signposted to Finlaggan: this is one of the most historic sites in Argyll and the short there-and-back detour is well worthwhile. Back on the route, the tarmac turns into gravel and once you enter the woodland things get muddy. It's worth

enduring the muddy track, as soon after the woodland the gravel track offers great views to Colonsay and Jura. From Bunnahabhain, the route follows the road for a while and connects through another short section with the road to Caol Ila, and then returns to Port Askaig.

After taking the ferry from Port Askaig to Kennacraig on the Kintyre peninsula, the route first follows the A83 and then a gravel road which climbs gradually uphill. Once at the top, take the first track on the left, which can be steep and technical at times. Passing the remains of Tarbert Castle, the route descends on the Kintyre Way into the small fishing village of Tarbert and continues on the road to the ferry terminal.

From the ferry stop in Portavadie follow Sustrans Route 75 towards Millhouse. A short but fun detour on the Cowal Way from here is recommended, before the Sustrans route is rejoined from Kames into Tighnabruaich and then along the shore of Loch Riddon around Argyll's Secret Coast to Stronafian, where it leaves the Sustrans route to follow roads towards Colintraive. Scotland's second shortest ferry journey takes you to Rhubodach on the Isle of Bute.

Follow the A886 south from the ferry terminal and just before Port Bannatyne take a road on the right. Shortly afterwards, the route follows the line of an old tramway on a multi-

user path to Ettrick Bay. A nice flowy trail follows the bay south and then connects with the road. Continue on the A844 south and then eastbound. At a fork, continue straight on to the B878 which heads to Rothesay. In Rothesay the route passes the castle and follows the High Street towards Serpentine Road, one of the most iconic road climbs in Scotland. After the hairpins the route follows a track on the left into a woodland and joins Eastlands Road down to the shore. The route follows the road along the shore to Ascog, where seals often bask in the sunshine on the nearby rocks.

Continue on Mount Stuart Road and follow the signs to the house. This Gothic Revival house (£), the seat of the Stuarts of Bute, is one of the highlights of this route. The route takes you past the house and out of the grounds on to Bruchag Road. Shortly afterwards, it joins a gravel track on the left which meets the road again and continues on to Kingarth. You follow the road along Kingarth Bay and then a path to the right at the edge of a woodland to connect with Plan Road. At a T-junction take a left and

continue on the road for a while until a gravel track branches off on the right. This beautiful track, the route of the West Island Way, takes you along open moorland and joins the B881 back towards Rothesay. The route rejoins Serpentine Road, this time in descent, and finishes at the ferry terminal.

The last part of the route starts at Wemyss Bay ferry terminal on the mainland. Shore Road is followed through the town before the route joins Sustrans Route 753 along the coast. After a while the route follows the road again, with a segregated cycle route for most of the way to Gourock railway station. Gourock is a good starting place for new adventures, either by catching the ferry to Dunoon and joining the Wild About Argyll Trail or Dunoon Dirt Dash (page 75) routes in this book, or simply take the train back to Glasgow after an adventure well done.

L–R: *Finlaggan, Islay; resting on a beach, Bute*
© *Maciek Tomiczek; Ben More, Mull.*

SPOTLIGHT JENNY GRAHAM

BIKEPACKING THE BOUNDARY OF ARGYLL

@jennygrahamis_

On Thursday 18 October 2018, Jenny Graham made history by becoming the fastest woman to circumnavigate the world by bike. She started in Berlin and returned 124 days later, beating the previous record by 20 days. Jenny, who lives in the Highlands, is the author of *Coffee First, Then the World* and is a GCN+ presenter. She joined Mark Beaumont, Markus Stitz and Maciek Tomiczek for the 2022 episode of the Explore Your Boundaries series.

'As a Scot, I know the north part of the country very well, but I've not explored very much down in Argyll. And every time I've been here, I've just been blown away by the coastline.

And I think that's the bit that gets me. When I think about Argyll, I just think of this rugged coastline and amazing beaches. And quite mixed weather, but atmospheric. It has always been atmospheric.

'Yesterday, when it was pouring down with rain first thing in the morning, that stuff doesn't really get to me. I just put my hood up, in the zone. Yeah, it was a big busy road, but it wasn't very busy with traffic. I was just churning away having a really nice chat with Mark, and I think that's all part of it. When you come to Scotland to go riding, then you're going to have mornings like that. And then you're going to be gifted with afternoons like

THE ROUTE

Explore Your Boundaries: Argyll and the Isles (*www.bikepackingscotland. com/boundaries*) is an 803-kilometre/499-mile bikepacking route, part of the Explore Your Boundaries project from Bikepacking Scotland.

Jenny's highlights of the route: '*Being in Southend. The cake had a lot to do with that. It was such good hospitality. But once we started heading back north, and we were on our way up to Tarbert on the east coast, that was just stunning. It was out of this world. There was no traffic on the roads and the beaches were gorgeous. The sun was out and we stopped at a distillery. Everyone was just in really high spirits and I really enjoyed that. But then I also enjoyed, on another trip, the Glen Etive area much further north. That's way more mountainous, and that's my natural habitat, the mountains.*'

VIDEO INSPIRATION

we had yesterday, when the sun came out. And every time we met each other at the top of the hill, we'd be like, wow!

'*An arbitrary route. You're sticking to it as much as you can. For no particular reason other than to see if you can do it. There's something very attractive to me about that, circumnavigating something and crossing something. I love looking back at the map and looking at my route and seeing that I've made a thing. I like the places that it takes you. It's quite often off the beaten track, so you're not just going to all the tourist places. And I like the challenge. We've been hiking with our bike, we've been dragging our bike over things that you just wouldn't normally bother doing. And then we've been completely gifted with views that we wouldn't normally get either. I like the places it takes you, and the challenges that it gives you. And the end result is that beautiful map.*'

L–R: On a cycle path near Tyndrum; gravel path in Glen Orchy; cakes at Muneroy Stores, Kintyre © Maciek Tomiczek; Jenny at Scalpsie Bay © Maciek Tomiczek.

14 AROUND LOCH AWE

INTRODUCTION

Nestled in the heart of mainland Argyll is Loch Awe, Scotland's longest freshwater loch spanning 41 kilometres of unspoilt, rugged and outstanding beauty. If you want to discover the magic of Scotland's temperate rainforest, ancient castles, crannogs and an abundance of gravel tracks, this loop is the perfect itinerary for a long weekend.

THE ROUTE

The route starts at Loch Awe railway station, which is frequently serviced by ScotRail's bike-friendly Highland Explorer. After a short climb you'll join the busy A85 for about 2.5 kilometres, passing Kilchurn Castle, one of the most photographed castles in Scotland. It was built in the 15th century and remained the base of the Campbells of Glenorchy for 150 years. The castle was converted into a garrison stronghold after the first Jacobite rising in 1689, but was abandoned by the end of the 18th century; it is currently closed to the public. Continuing along the A819 shortly afterwards you will get a great view of the castle from the lay-by on the road, or an even better view by walking across the grassland to the shore.

Shortly after the lay-by the route follows a smooth and wide gravel track to meet the public road towards the Duncan Ban Macintyre Monument. The monument celebrates one of the most renowned Scottish Gaelic poets and offers great views across the area and over to Argyll's highest mountain, Ben Cruachan. You descend on the Old Military Road through a stunning Atlantic woodland to meet the A819 again at Achlian. This will give you a first taste of the many amazing woodlands you will come across on this loop. Loch Awe is a home to Scotland's temperate rainforest, with ancient oak, ash, birch,

ROUTE CONDITIONS
· Singletrack: 1%
· Path: 33%
· Road: 66%
· Recommended bike: gravel bike

Track near Sròn Mhòr above the shores of Loch Awe.

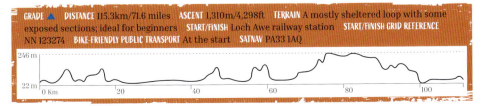

GRADE ▲ DISTANCE 115.3km/71.6 miles ASCENT 1,310m/4,298ft TERRAIN A mostly sheltered loop with some exposed sections; ideal for beginners START/FINISH Loch Awe railway station START/FINISH GRID REFERENCE NN 123274 BIKE-FRIENDLY PUBLIC TRANSPORT At the start SATNAV PA33 1AQ

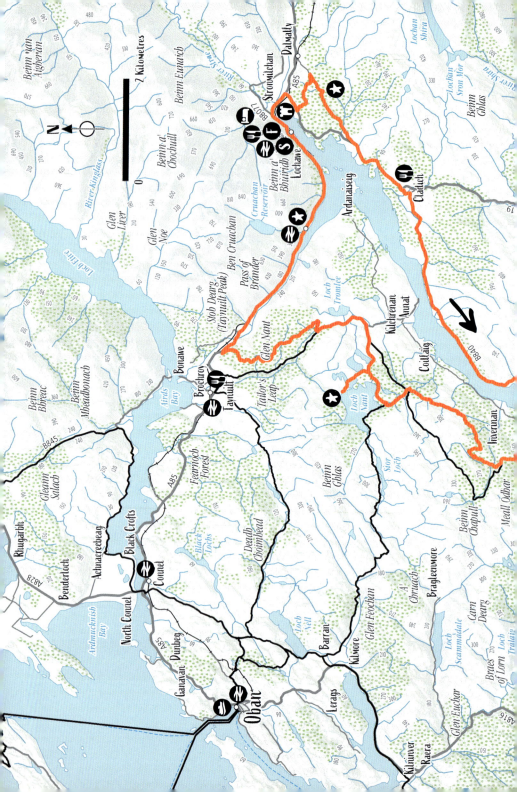

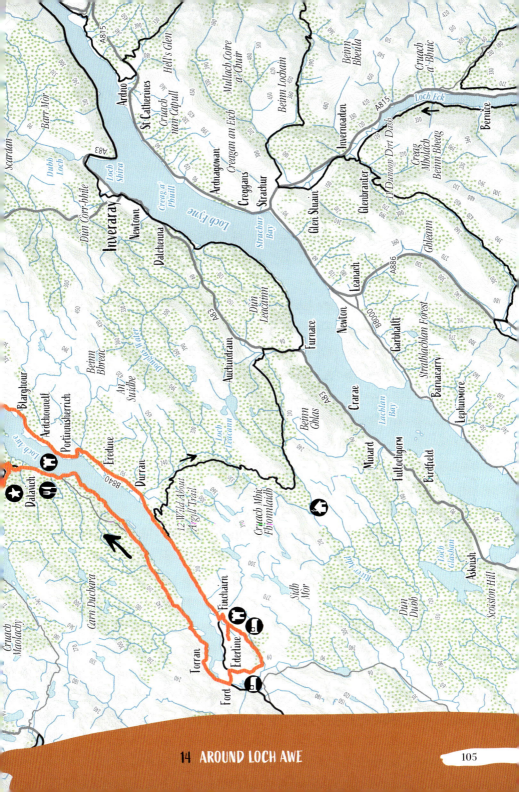

hazel and Scots pine trees. This part of Scotland sees a fair bit of rain, which makes cycling through the woodlands even more interesting: if you are travelling between May and September, make sure you cover yourself sufficiently as there are plenty of midges and ticks to be found here.

The route continues on the A819 until Cladich, from where it continues on the B840, a much quieter and more enjoyable singletrack road. Shortly after Cladich you'll pass Cakes in the Call Box, a converted red telephone box where local resident Holly serves lovely home-made cakes and jams with an honesty box. The route continues on the quiet road past Ardbrecknish House, where you can hire canoes and boats from Loch Awe Boats, and Portsonachan Hotel. From here the route undulates along the beautiful shore of Loch Awe, passing dense woodlands, waterfalls and a few houses. Make sure to stop and marvel at Innis Chonnel Castle, one of the earliest Campbell strongholds from as early as the 14th century. The island on which it is sited and the adjacent shore are now heavily wooded, but you can get a good glimpse of the castle's remains from the shore. A bit further south the remains of a chapel are situated on a small island, Innis Errich.

The route continues on the road through more stunning woodlands to Eredine. There are several opportunities to pitch your tent on this stretch, and at a nearby parking place a gravel track climbs up the hill: this is where the Wild About Argyll Trail (page 81) leaves the shore of Loch Awe. If you are looking to extend your adventure, take this track up to Tom Soilleir, from where a rough track leads to Carron bothy. Alternatively, continue on the road to Finchairn and take a gravel track to the left up the hill just after a house. To the right you will find a gate and a track over a field that leads to the very ruinous remains of Fincharn Castle, which stands on a rocky promontory. This is the oldest castle on this loop, possibly first built as early as 1240.

The track climbs towards a hill, and the short detour to the remains of a medieval parish church dedicated to St Columba is worthwhile. It's hard to spot from the track: look out for an iron gate. You'll find the remains with an oratory in the churchyard – this was still in use as a burial ground at the end

WHEN TO RIDE
This route is good all year round.

WARNINGS
The first and final stretches on the A85 can be busy with traffic.

FOOD AND DRINK
· Ben Cruachan Inn, Lochawe.
  T: 01838 200 880
· Cakes in the Call Box, near Cladich.
· Kilmartin Hotel, Kilmartin (detour).
  T: 01546 510 250
· Wild Rowan Cafe, Dalavich.
  T: 01866 844 256
· The Robin's Nest, Taynuilt (detour).
  T: 01866 822 429

ACCOMMODATION
· Ben Cruachan Inn, Lochawe.
  T: 01838 200 880
· Ederline Estate Guest House, Ford.
  T: 01546 810 284
· Crown House Bed and Breakfast, Ford.
  T: 01546 810 279

L–R: *Kilchurn Castle; Innis Chonnel Castle; Avich Falls.*

OTHER ROUTES NEARBY

· Wild About Argyll Trail (page 81) and Bikepacking Argyll's Islands (page 91).
· Caledonia Way (parts are on Sustrans Route 78) – www.visitscotland.com

BIKE SHOPS AND HIRE

· Rusty Cycle Shed, Taynuilt (shop, hire). T: 07791 974 152

VIDEO INSPIRATION

L–R: Loch an Leòid; descending from Loch Nant into Glen Nant.

of the 19th century. The views over Loch Awe from the top of the hill are superb, but this section of the route can get muddy. The descent takes you through the Ederline Estate, which has an excellent B & B as an overnight option. You'll meet the road again just before Ford, at the most southerly point of Loch Awe. There is another excellent B & B in Ford, Crown House, whose owners Pete and Sue offer a free shuttle service to the nearby Kilmartin Hotel for food. You can also continue south from here on the Caledonia Way, or join the Bikepacking Argyll's Islands route (page 91).

Your route continues on the road on the western shore of Loch Awe, following the Caledonia Way. At Kilmaha a gravel track takes you down to the shore, avoiding one of the many hills on this road. Approximately halfway along you'll find a turn-off to the site of a crannog on the right, and shortly afterwards a waymarked walk climbs up through MacKenzie's Grove with its giant Douglas fir trees. You'll rejoin the road to Dalavich at Newyork. The cafe in Dalavich is a great place to stop, and the Dalavich Social Club offers evening meals and a bar, and camping spots and pods.

At Barnaline the route follows a small singletrack through a majestic Atlantic oakwood, before climbing to Avich Falls, one of the most impressive waterfalls in Scotland. The route

continues on a track to Loch Avich, before continuing on a gravel 'highway' through Gleann Meisean. There is an abundance of forestry roads on the western side of Loch Awe, and therefore many alternatives to the route described here if you are feeling adventurous. Watch out for heavy logging trucks, though – this is an active forest with an ever-expanding wind farm nearby. The route continues on a variety of gravel tracks, with great views over Loch Awe once you reach a big clearing. More gravel tracks lead to the beautiful Loch Nant, where a road is followed to the Loch Nant Dam, and back again. If you are short for time and dams are of little interest, you can skip this short section.

After passing two more lochs, the route descends on a wind farm service road to the B845. Expect more climbing and stunning views. After approximately two kilometres, your route follows a track on the right to Shellachan, but you can also continue on the Caledonia Way along the road. This is a beautiful gravel track through the forest on the northern edges of Glen Nant, first climbing gently and then descending to meet the A85 after Taynuilt. The next section on the A85 can be busy with traffic, and so you have two options: take a left to head into Taynuilt and take the train home or to the finish of the route from there, or continue on the A85 through the Pass of Brander, passing the Cruachan Power Station where you can discover the cavernous machine hall and turbines hidden deep within Ben Cruachan. Although cycling on the main road is not ideal, the scenery here is reminiscent of a Norwegian fjord. A stop at St Conan's Kirk in the village of Lochawe is a must. The kirk, designed and built by Walter Douglas Campbell, is unique in that it features almost every style of church architecture you can find. You can finish your ride with a beer and dinner at the Ben Cruachan Inn, or follow the service road up to the mighty Cruachan Dam and back if you still have juice left in your legs.

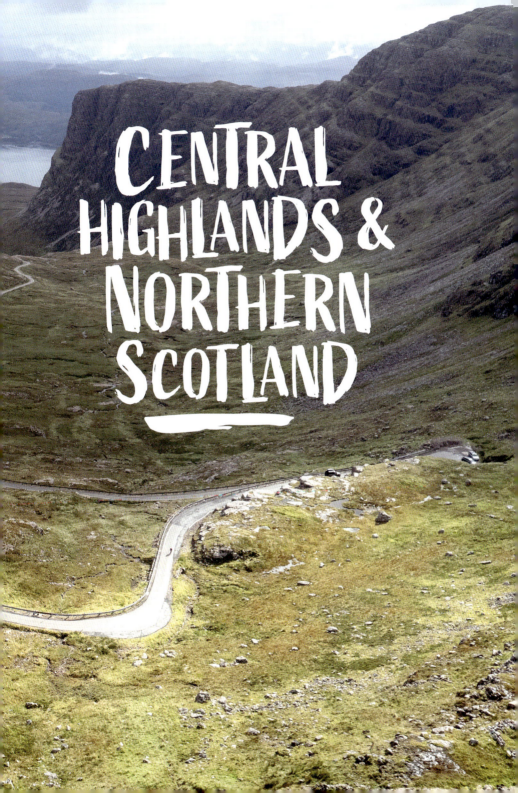

CENTRAL HIGHLANDS & NORTHERN SCOTLAND

15 HIGHLAND PERTHSHIRE DROVERS TRAIL

INTRODUCTION

This is one of the key routes of the Perthshire Gravel trails which were developed in 2020. It's an enjoyable off-road journey steeped in history which passes through a wide variety of Scottish landscapes and small market towns and villages. This bikepacking epic features the remote and scenic glens of the Cairngorms National Park; the Tay, Scotland's longest river; Scotland's smallest and oldest distilleries; the last surviving oak tree from the wood that inspired Shakespeare's *Macbeth*; waterfalls that heartened Robert Burns; General Wade's Military Roads; drove roads; and some of the best gravel paths that the Highlands have to offer.

THE ROUTE

The route starts in Pitlochry, a Victorian town which became a tourism destination after a visit from Queen Victoria and Prince Albert in 1842. Pitlochry has excellent rail connections and is on Sustrans National Cycle Network Route 7. From the centre, the route follows quiet roads to Moulin. The Moulin Hotel, also the starting point for the A tour of Highland Perthshire route from *Great British Gravel Rides*, has been inviting visitors for three centuries and is a popular stop for cyclists for food and refreshments. From here the route crosses a field past the ruins of Black Castle, so named due to its abandonment in fear of the plague in the 16th century. A network of small walking paths is followed to Milton of Edradour, with Edradour distillery, the smallest distillery in Scotland, just a few hundred metres off the route. From here you follow the A924 to Straloch and to the southern end of Gleann Fearnach; the route overlaps here with the Cairngorms

ROUTE CONDITIONS
- Singletrack: 7%
- Path: 57%
- Cycle path: 1%
- Road: 35%
- Recommended bike: gravel or mountain bike

Previous page: *The famous switch-backs of the Bealach na Bà, Applecross* (route 20).

Riding on an old drovers' route from Ardtalnaig to Comrie.

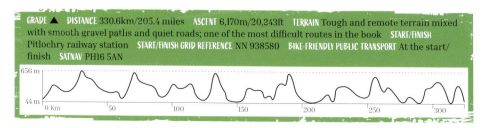

GRADE ▲ **DISTANCE** 330.6km/205.4 miles **ASCENT** 6,170m/20,243ft **TERRAIN** Tough and remote terrain mixed with smooth gravel paths and quiet roads; one of the most difficult routes in the book **START/FINISH** Pitlochry railway station **START/FINISH GRID REFERENCE** NN 938580 **BIKE-FRIENDLY PUBLIC TRANSPORT** At the start/finish **SATNAV** PH16 5AN

656 m

44 m

0 Km   50   100   150   200   250   300

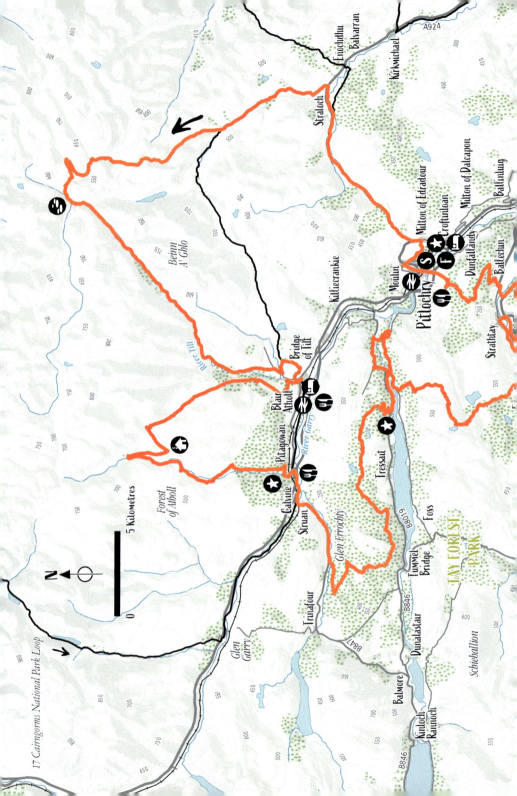

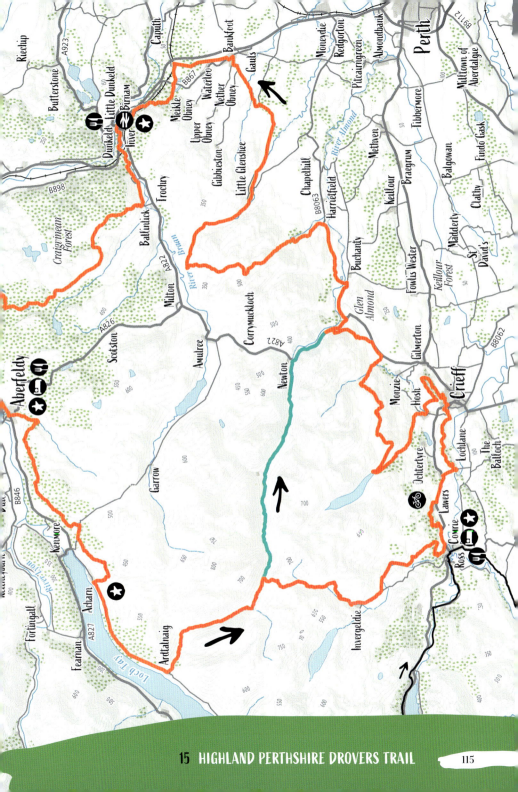

BIKEPACKING SCOTLAND

National Park Loop (page 131). A smooth tarmac road turns into a well-maintained gravel track at Daldhu, and from here the glen narrows and the gradients become steeper until a pass at 656 metres, the highest point on the entire route.

The good gravel track ends at Fealar Lodge, where the going gets much tougher. Although a track is often clearly visible, some of it is over boggy upland and requires pushing the bike. Upon leaving the plateau, a washed-out path descends steeply towards the River Tilt. Note that crossing the river can be dangerous after heavy rainfall. Heading south the track gradually improves until reaching the Falls of Tarf, and both the falls and Bedford Bridge are impressive landmarks. From here the route continues through Glen Tilt, often described as one of the most beautiful glens in Scotland, and after a pretty technical section the route uses a well-maintained doubletrack to Marble Lodge. Cross the river on a bridge and shortly afterwards you climb on a grassy track on the eastern side of Auchghobal towards Fenderbridge. The turn-off, easy to miss, is marked with a small yellow arrow on a wooden post. Just before reaching the hamlet, the route joins a small tarmac road. The route passes through Fenderbridge and continues on a small road.

The route descends to the B8079 at Blair Atholl and almost immediately follows a small path back north along the River Tilt to Old Bridge of Tilt, from where it continues for a short section on tarmac to Old Blair. From Old Blair, a well-maintained gravel track climbs steadily north, following Allt Slanaidh past Càrn Dearg Mòr, reaching the highest point at over 630 metres before descending on a washed-out and rough track through Allt Scheicheachan to the MBA bothy with the same name. This small bothy is an ideal place to spend the night or shelter from bad weather. After crossing the stream, the route follows a very boggy footpath north through deep heather towards Glen Bruar: for most, this will be a straight push all the way to Bruar Lodge. Here, join a well-maintained gravel track, cross the river and head south. At a fork, marked by a private hut, the route leaves the smooth gravel again to cross the Bruar Water and continues over open moorland before joining a good forestry

WHEN TO RIDE
With some exposed terrain, this ride is at its best between April and November.

WARNINGS
The track from Fealar Lodge is very tough where a washed-out path descends steeply towards the river. Note that crossing the river can be dangerous after heavy rainfall.

L–R: *Burns statue at the Birks of Aberfeldy; Glenturret distillery, the oldest in Scotland; looking over to Ben Chonzie; Glen Tilt.*

FOOD AND DRINK

- Escape Route Cafe, Pittochry.
  T: 01796 473 859
- Moulin Hotel, Pittochry.
  T: 01796 472 196
- Wasted Degrees Taproom (Saturdays April to October), Blair Atholl –
  www.wasteddegrees.com
- The Bothy Bar, Atholl Arms Hotel, Blair Atholl. T: 01796 481 205
- House of Bruar, Bruar.
  T: 01796 483 236
- The Grandtully Hotel by Ballintaggart, Grandtully. T: 01887 447 000
- Aberfeldy Watermill Bookshop & Cafe, Aberfeldy. T: 01887 822 896
- The Tea Garden at Comrie Croft, Comrie. T: 01764 670 140
- The Scottish Deli, Dunkeld.
  T: 01350 728 028

track at the top of Glen Banvie to the Falls of Bruar. Upon reaching a lookout, a walking trail zigzags through the forest and crosses the Falls of Bruar at an old stone bridge, with a few steps afterwards. From the House of Bruar, a popular stop for food and country clothing, the route follows Sustrans Route 7 to Calvine and joins the B847 towards Kinloch Rannoch, crossing the River Garry shortly after the turn-off. The road follows the Errochty Water through a stunning valley. Halfway through, a smooth wide track climbs gradually into forest, followed by another wide gravel track towards Loch Bhac through the Tay Forest Park. From here the route descends through Allean Forest towards the Queen's View above Loch Tummel. The lookout is said to be named after Queen Victoria, following her visit to the area in 1866, and is home to one of Scotland's most remarkable views.

You follow the B8019 on the northern side of Loch Tummel, passing Bonskeid House. Shortly afterwards, a gravel track heads south towards the river, where you leave the track at a clearing, crossing on a singletrack beneath pylons to finally reach the Coronation Bridge, a suspension footbridge over the River Tummel. From here you join the road south of the river to Netherton, where a steep track climbs south past Duntanlich Lochan and heads west towards its highest point near Beinn Eagagach, crossing the Duntanlich Mine Road. Past Loch Derculich the route descends on well-maintained farm tracks and minor tarmac roads to join Sustrans Route 7 near Cluny House Gardens, a secluded, unique woodland garden overlooking the Strath Tay valley. You follow the Sustrans route and cross the River Tay between Strathtay and Grandtully, and then continue on an old railway line towards Aberfeldy. Near Pitcairn Church the wide path narrows to continue along

the river to Dewar's Aberfeldy Distillery. From here the route follows the A827 into Aberfeldy. Famous for its mention in the poem 'The Birks of Aberfeldy' by Robert Burns, the small market town is also known for its Wade Bridge, built in 1733.

Turning south in the centre of town on the A826, the route shortly afterwards follows a footpath on the western side of the Moness Burn through the Birks of Aberfeldy. Originally called the Den of Moness, the birks – from the Scots for birch trees – line the slopes of the Moness gorge. Some sections are steep, and near the top there are a few wooden steps and a small bridge that require getting off the bike and pushing. The route then follows the Rob Roy Way on the southern side of the River Tay, with spectacular views towards Schiehallion and Ben Lawers. Joining the road towards Kenmore, the route shortly afterwards continues on a forest track and then on a landrover track known as the Queen's Drive, named in memory of Queen Victoria's visit to the area in the 19th century. It leads to the Falls of Acharn, situated in a spectacular wooded gorge. You follow the Queen's Drive on the western side of the falls, where a small man-made cavern, known as the Hermit's Cave, is a great spot to stop. The route continues on Sustrans Route 7 on the South Loch Tay road to Ardtalnaig.

From Ardtalnaig you follow a former drove road to Comrie. A smooth tarmac road follows Gleann a' Chilleine east and soon turns into a rough road at Claggan, turning south and climbing further to Dunan, a small, private stalkers' hut. The route continues on the northern side of the river until a small dam is reached, where either the ford or the dam provide an opportunity to cross. You can shortcut the route here by continuing on the gravel track through the glen to Newton Bridge. Next is the most difficult and remote section

ACCOMMODATION

- Pitlochry Youth Hostel, Pitlochry. T: 01796 472 308
- Pitlochry Backpackers Hotel, Pitlochry. T: 01796 470 044
- Blair Castle Caravan Park, Blair Atholl. T: 01796 481 263
- Schiehallion Hotel, Aberfeldy. T: 01887 820 421
- Comrie Croft, Comrie. T: 01764 670 140

OTHER ROUTES NEARBY

- Cairngorms National Park Loop (page 131) and A Scottish Hostelling Adventure (page 151).
- A Tour of Highland Perthshire – www.adventurebooks.com/gbgr
- Perthshire Gravel Trails – www.perthshiregravel.com
- Sustrans National Cycle Network routes 7 and 77 – www.sustrans.org.uk
- Cairngorms Loop – www.cairngormsloop.net
- Cateran Ecomuseum routes – www.cateranecomuseum.co.uk

L–R: *On the shores of Loch Tay; climbing to the highest point of the route in Gleann Fearnach.*

BIKE SHOPS AND HIRE

- Escape Route, Pitlochry (shop, hire).
  T: 01796 473 859
- Beyond Adventure, Aberfeldy (hire).
  T: 01887 829 202
- Draft & Flow, Aberfeldy (shop).
  T: 07457 403 845
- Highland Safaris, Dull (hire).
  T: 01887 820 071
- Comrie Croft Bikes (shop, hire).
  T: 01764 670 140
- Progression Bikes, Dunkeld (shop,
  hire). T: 01350 727 629

NOTES

If you want to swap pedals for paddles, Outdoor Explore offers great guided kayaking, canoeing, stand-up paddle-boarding and coracle adventures.
www.outdoorexplore.co.uk

VIDEO INSPIRATION

of the route: it requires good navigation skills, especially in poor visibility. A steep landrover track climbs to about 600 metres, where the route leaves the track and crosses the moor to the pass (bealach) at 633 metres. Reaching the bealach, a good track follows on the west side of the Invergeldie Burn to Coishavachan, where the route continues on a quiet public road down Glen Lednock. At Funtulich, you leave the road again and continue through farmland to reach the northern bank of the River Lednock. Crossing a small stream you reach a landrover track, passing Balmuick Cottages. The track continues and meets the River Lednock again, and from here the route follows a walking path to Comrie, a village on the southern border of the Scottish Highlands. Comrie's geological position on the Highland Boundary Fault has caused it to experience more earth tremors than anywhere else in Scotland. You can see a replica of the world's first seismometer, installed in 1874, at the tiny Earthquake House nearby at Ross. This route also meets the A Scottish Hostelling Adventure route (page 151) in Comrie.

The route passes on the eastern edge of the village and follows the A85 to a caravan park, where it leaves the busy road and follows a path through an alley of giant redwood trees. You then follow good gravel tracks to Comrie Croft, which has a great network of mountain bike trails. From here the route rejoins the A85 for a brief stretch eastbound. Shortly after Carse of Trowan the route follows a minor road to the right, and then climbs on forest paths over a few hills and past a small lochan to Crieff. Throughout medieval times, Crieff was a major political and judicial centre, and developed into the main cattle trading centre in Scotland between the 16th and 18th centuries. Drovers and up to 30,000 black cattle would converge on the huge livestock market.

L–R: *Moulin Inn awaits cyclists with a warm welcome; following Allt Slanaidh past Càrn Dearg Mòr.*

Following paths and quiet roads through town the route passes Crieff Hydro Hotel and then follows a well-maintained gravel track around the Knock of Crieff. You then descend on a singletrack to Glenturret distillery, the oldest in Scotland. Following the Turret Burn, the route climbs on tarmac to Loch Turret Reservoir. Robert Burns' visit here in 1787 inspired him to write his poem 'A Wild Scene Among the Hills of Oughtertyre'. The route follows a gravel track through a stunning upland landscape to join the A822 at the Falls of Monzie, and then traces General Wade's Military Road to rejoin the A822 at Sma' Glen; the earlier shortcut from Dunan rejoins the main route here. In the early 18th century, cattle drovers would travel through Sma' Glen from Loch Tay on their journey to the market at Crieff.

From Sma' Glen you continue on the B8063 east along the River Almond. At Milton Farm the route leaves the tarmac to climb north alongside the Milton Burn before descending Glen Shee south then east on landrover tracks and quiet roads towards the small village of Bankfoot. From here the route follows a mixture of good tracks and paths towards the Pass of Birnam, and alongside the railway line to Birnam; the last section is on a technical singletrack through the forest. An alternative route crosses the railway line at Birnam Quarry and joins the Salmon Run, Sustrans Route 77, towards the railway station. Home of the World Haggis Eating Competition, Dunkeld and Birnam are two villages on the banks of the River Tay, linked by a bridge built by Thomas Telford in 1809. Birnam, on the south bank of the Tay, is home to the Birnam Oak, mentioned in Shakespeare's *Macbeth*. Dunkeld, on the north bank of the Tay, has a cathedral, and around 20 of the houses within Dunkeld have been restored by the National Trust for Scotland.

After Dunkeld the route passes through The Hermitage under giant Douglas firs – among the tallest trees in Britain – to Ossian's Hall of Mirrors, a good place to spot salmon jumping up the Black Linn Falls of the River Braan. Leaving the woodland the route follows Wade's Military Road on a small tarmac road to Ballinlick, before it climbs steeply on a gravel track to Griffin Wind Farm. Following gravel roads the route then joins the forest, where a short hike-a-bike section through a very boggy clearing connects two service roads. From here the route descends past the hillfort of Castle Dow to join the B898 and Sustrans Route 7 to cross the River Tay near Pitnacree. Heading briefly east on the A827, the route then climbs up a very good gravel road into Ballechin Wood. Following an access road for the Duntanlich Mine, the route crosses the A9 south of the town and follows cycle paths and quiet roads back to Pitlochry.

SPOTLIGHT ALAN GOLDSMITH

ENCOURAGING AN EQUAL GENDER SPLIT AT THE HIGHLAND TRAIL 550
@ht550alan

Alan Goldsmith is the creator of the Highland Trail 550, the most popular bikepacking event in Scotland. He organises the mass-start event each May on a voluntary basis. There are no prizes – all that is provided is inspiration, a suggested start time, a GPX file and a list of completion times. In 2023, the start list for the event features women and men in equal proportion, and riders need to make a donation to the John Muir Trust, a nature conservation charity for which Alan raised over £4,000 at the previous event.

'For the 2023 edition of the Highland Trail 550 I have made it my number one priority to have a 50–50 gender split on the start list. In the first edition in 2013 there were no women at all. The following year there was one, Iona Evans. After that it increased in ones and twos for a few years, before a big surge in 2022 when 17 women took to the start, and for a while the start list was actually up to 25. The steep increase is mostly down to inspirational women like Annie Le, Jenny Graham, Lee Craigie and Gail Brown leading by example and showing what is possible. Annie was the first person to complete the route in winter, something I previously thought would never be done.

'I wanted to keep the steep rise in interest going for 2023, so I have been proactive in encouraging women to sign up. I set a target of 30 women, but have gone beyond that now with 35 on the start list. I even have a waiting list with a few more women ready to replace anyone that drops out. Hopefully, this year will

THE ROUTE

The Highland Trail 550 (*www.highlandtrail550. weebly.com*) is an 885-kilometre/550-mile self-supported mountain bike time trial route through the Scottish Highlands.

Alan's highlight of the route: '*My route highlight is – predictably enough – Fisherfield. Also known as the Great Wilderness, this entire section is stunning, but if I had to pick one location, it would be the hairpin bends just before the descent to the Causeway. The view from there is truly awe-inspiring, and despite having been there ten times over the years, it never fails to take my breath away. In the last two editions of Highland Trail 550 I have made the decision to stop early and camp out in Fisherfield rather than rushing on through. I never regret lingering in this very special place; memorable moments are more important to me now than trimming a few hours off my finishing time. For me this is undoubtedly the Queen Stage of the Highland Trail 550.*'

not be a one-off and the trend will continue in the coming years and other bikepacking events will also strive for equal gender ratios at the start.

'I have also given up flying for good; my last flight was in 2019 (a short-haul return to Slovenia) and that was my only flight in the last ten years. I decided to raise awareness of personal environmental impact to riders in future editions of the Highland Trail 550. GBDURO's sustainability ethos showed me what you can do if you have the time and motivation. In 2023, I will be encouraging all riders to arrive in Tyndrum in the least harmful way they can, be it riding, train or, at the very least, ride sharing. I will also select fewer overseas riders, limiting these to ten with only two or three from outside Europe. In the past, I've seen that often riders from outside Europe have a family connection in Scotland and are combining the trip to visit relatives, which slightly helps my eco-sensitive conscience.'

VIDEO INSPIRATION

16 THE CATERAN GRAN FONDO

INTRODUCTION

Stretching from the Valley of Strathmore into the southern edge of the Cairngorms National Park, the Cateran Ecomuseum is characterised by quiet roads and beautiful scenery. All of the museum's sites are free and outside. This road cycling loop, just a few kilometres short of the official Gran Fondo distance, takes you past some of the key points of interest and through breathtaking Highland and Lowland scenery, with multiple opportunities to stop and soak in the views, or to enjoy a good cup of coffee.

THE ROUTE

This loop starts at Alyth Market Square. For centuries Alyth was an important market town on the drove roads, along which farmers brought sheep and cattle to lowland markets. The route follows a number of small roads through the small Perthshire town and on the way out passes Alyth's Pack Bridge, one of the oldest masonry bridges in Scotland, and the Den o' Alyth, a wooded glen. Much of the stone to build parts of Alyth in earlier times was quarried from this glen. Shortly afterwards you will pass Bamff Estate, an upland farm which has been pioneering environmental restoration since the 1980s, including the successful reintroduction of beavers in 2002.

From Bamff, the route follows the Cateran Trail, climbing steadily to Park Neuk stone circle. Just a short walk off the road this small four-poster stone circle is beautifully set on the north-eastern shoulder of a low hill. At Burnside of Drimmie the Cateran Trail continues off-road, while this route stays on the road to Cloquhat, where the Cateran Trail rejoins. The descent into Netherton is followed by a short but sharp climb to Bridge of Cally, a small settlement on the banks of the confluence of

ROUTE CONDITIONS
· Road: 100%
· Recommended bike: road bike

WHEN TO RIDE
This road route is good all year round.

WARNINGS
The section on the A93 can be busy with traffic.

Trevor Ward en route to Balintore Castle.

GRADE ▲	DISTANCE 109km/67.7 miles	ASCENT 1,050m/3,445ft	TERRAIN Mostly quiet roads through mountainous landscapes	START/FINISH Alyth Market Square	START/FINISH GRID REFERENCE NO 246485	BIKE-FRIENDLY

PUBLIC TRANSPORT Apollo Way bus stop, Dundee, 24.2km from the start/finish   SATNAV PH11 8AA

401 m

34 m

0 Km   20   40   60   80   100

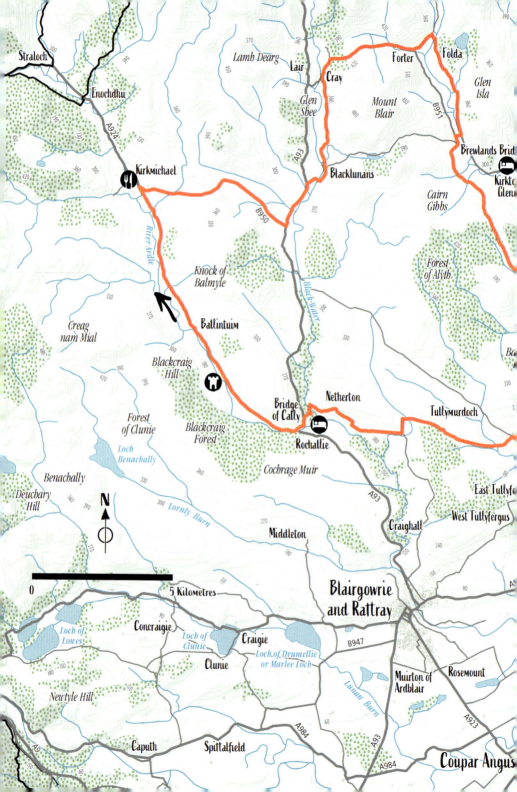

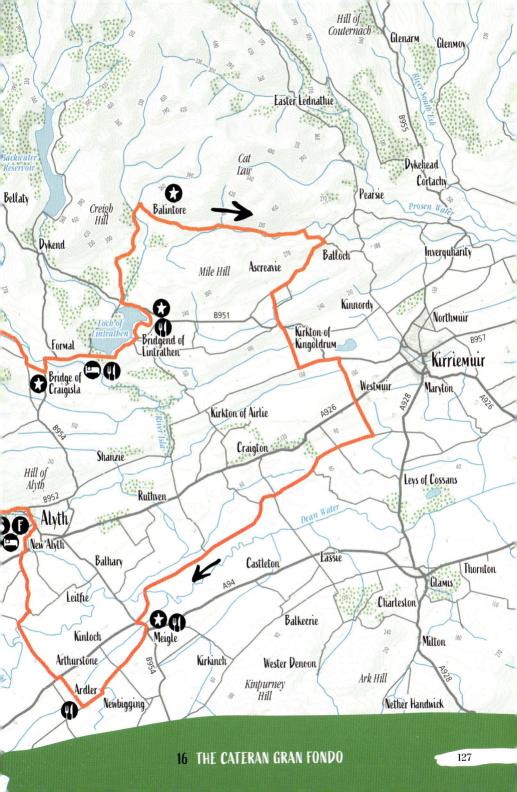

FOOD AND DRINK

· The Barony, Alyth. T: 07871 309 900
· Kirkmichael Village Shop, Kirkmichael.
  T: 01250 881 272
· Glenisla Hotel, Kirkton of Glenisla
  (detour). T: 01575 582 366
· Peel Farm Coffee Shop, Lintrathen.
  T: 01575 560 205
· Wee Bear Cafe, Lintrathen.
  T: 01575 560 477
· Flour Coffee Shop & Deli, Meigle.
  T: 01828 640 610
· The Joinery Coffee Shop, Meigle.
  T: 01828 640 717
· The Ardler Tavern, Ardler.
  T: 01828 640 037

NOTES

Jane Wilkinson from Special Branch
Baskets is based in the Ecomuseum
and offers coracle building courses.
A coracle is a one-person boat
made out of woven wood and
with a waterproof covering.
www.specialbranchbaskets.com

L–R: *Park Neuk stone circle; the road
from Brewlands to Kilry; forest at
Bamff.*

the rivers Ericht and Ardle.

The River Ardle is followed upstream on the busier A924,
passing Blackcraig Castle, Ballintuim and the impressive
Balnabroich standing stone. This single standing stone, dating
from the Neolithic or Bronze Age, is often used by cattle as
a rubbing post, so you have to look closely to spot it. At the
junction of the A924 and B950 an ornate Celtic monument
made of Aberdeenshire granite commemorates James Small,
an important 19th-century Scottish laird from Kirkmichael.
The village itself is only a short detour from the intersection.
From here the quieter B950 leads over a ridge and into the next
valley, joining the A93 and the SnowRoads scenic route for a
short section at Dalrulzion, before a small road follows the
Black Water from Drumfork to Blair House, passing a church
at Cray. The route continues on the B951, also becoming the
Cateran Trail shortly afterwards, to skirt around the northern
side of Mount Blair, a prominent hill. First climbing steadily,
the route then descends into the picturesque Glen Isla, passing
Forter Castle, originally built in 1560 by James Ogilvy and
rebuilt in the early 1990s.

After the Forter Bridge over the River Isla the route leaves
the Cateran Trail again and takes the quieter road on the
eastern side of the river through Folda. While not suitable for
any bikes with skinnier tyres, it is possible to connect here with
the In search of gravel on the Monega Pass route from *Great
British Gravel Rides*. You cross the River Isla again at Brewlands
on the new bridge built in 1970, getting a sight of the scenic old
bridge which replaced treacherous stepping stones 50 metres
downstream. From here a big climb follows to the highest point
of the route near Druim Dearg. The views north from the top
are breathtaking. This quiet road continues over a few cattle

grids before descending to Kilry and on to Bridge of Craigisla.

Parking the bike and taking a short walk to Reekie Linn, one of Scotland's most spectacular waterfalls, is highly recommended. The route continues past two great coffee stops at Peel Farm and Bridgend of Lintrathen, and around the wildlife reserve Loch of Lintrathen. The reserve is home to breeding songbirds in summer, while in winter large numbers of wintering birds such as greylag geese visit the area. The two hides on the banks of the loch make for fine viewing points.

From the loch a small road climbs north towards Balintore Castle, which can already be seen from a good distance away. Commissioned as a shooting lodge in the late 1800s by David Lyon, a slave owner and parliamentarian, the castle occupies an elevated site in moorland above Balintore village. The design is typical of the Scottish Baronial style, and after being abandoned in the 1960s it is now being privately restored. After the castle the route continues east for a while along the upper reaches of the valley, before descending steeply towards Auldallan and the beautiful valley alongside the Quharity Burn. After another climb, Kirkton of Kingoldrum is reached, from where the route descends into the Valley of Strathmore.

The route travels westbound on mostly flat roads through extensive farmland, with Meigle and Ardler providing great opportunities to stop. The Meigle Sculptured Stone Museum (£) is home to a magnificent collection of carved stones, some of which date back to the late eighth century. All found in Meigle, mostly in the churchyard or built into the church, they are all that survives of a centre of Pictish wealth and patronage. Shortly after crossing the River Isla a final climb leads back to the start in Alyth.

ACCOMMODATION

- Vanora's Cottages, Alyth. T: 07914 375 226
- Bridge of Cally Hotel. T: 0333 344 6612
- Glenisla Hotel, Kirkton of Glenisla (detour). T: 01575 582 366
- Peel Farm Glamping Pods, Lintrathen. T: 01575 560 205

OTHER ROUTES NEARBY

- Cateran Ecomuseum trails – www.cateranecomuseum.co.uk
- Cateran Trail – www.caterantrail.org
- SnowRoads scenic route – www.snowroads.com
- In search of gravel on the Monega Pass – www.adventurebooks.com/gbgr

BIKE SHOPS AND HIRE

- Alyth Cyclery, Alyth (shop). T: 07871 309 900
- Lintrathen Cycles, Bridgend of Lintrathen (hire). T: 01575 560 450

VIDEO INSPIRATION

17 CAIRNGORMS NATIONAL PARK LOOP

INTRODUCTION

The Cairngorms National Park is home to a quarter of Scotland's native forest and over a quarter of the UK's endangered species. Half of the Cairngorms has been recognised as being of international importance for nature. This route follows old military and drovers roads through the UK's largest area of high ground, regarded as climatically, geomorphologically and biologically the most extensive 'Arctic' area in the UK. While the Cairngorms is home to five of the six highest mountains in Scotland, there are no extreme climbs and descents on this route and parts of it can make for great day trips.

THE ROUTE

The route starts at Aviemore railway station, which is well-connected by ScotRail, LNER and Caledonian Sleeper services. It initially follows the Old Logging Way to the Old Bridge Inn, which is an excellent stop for food. Shortly afterwards, the route continues on the newest section of the Speyside Way. One of Scotland's Great Trails, the entire route of this long-distance route extends south from the Spey Bay at Buckie on the Moray coastline to Newtonmore. After a short section on and next to the B9152, the route leaves the road, passes a bridge and continues on a gravel path between the River Spey and the railway line through a mixture of farm and woodland. The constant up and down makes for fun riding, but factor in some extra time for this section of the Speyside Way. Adding time for a coffee stop at the Old Post Office in Kincraig is a must too. Note that the next stop for food from here is the House of Bruar, 58 kilometres away.

From Kincraig, the route continues on the Speyside Way, with some shorter sections following the signposted Badenoch

ROUTE CONDITIONS

- Singletrack: 10%
- Path: 44%
- Cycle Path: 6%
- Road: 40%
- Recommended bike: gravel bike

Glen Tromie.

GRADE ▲   DISTANCE 267.5km/166.2 miles   ASCENT 3,370m/11,056ft   TERRAIN A great mix of smooth gravel tracks, singletrack and mostly quiet roads   START/FINISH Aviemore railway station   START/FINISH GRID REFERENCE NH 895123   BIKE-FRIENDLY PUBLIC TRANSPORT At the start/finish   SATNAV PH22 1PD

670 m

219 m

0 Km   50   100   150   200   250

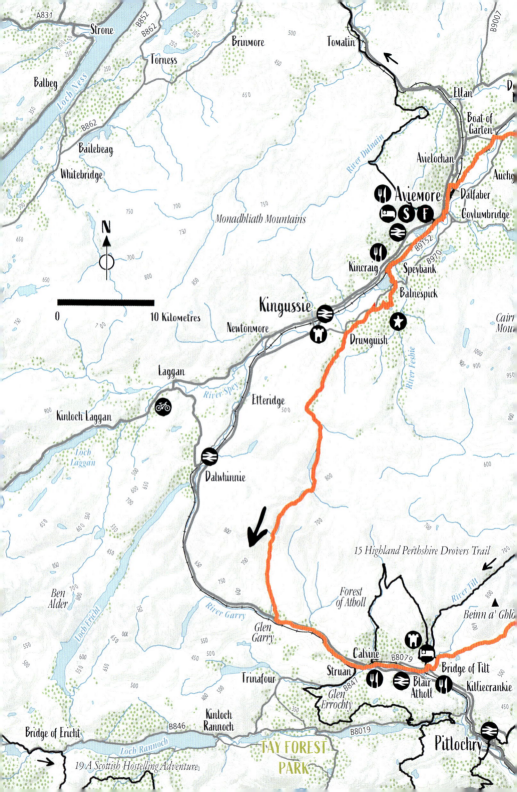

15 Highland Perthshire Drovers Trail

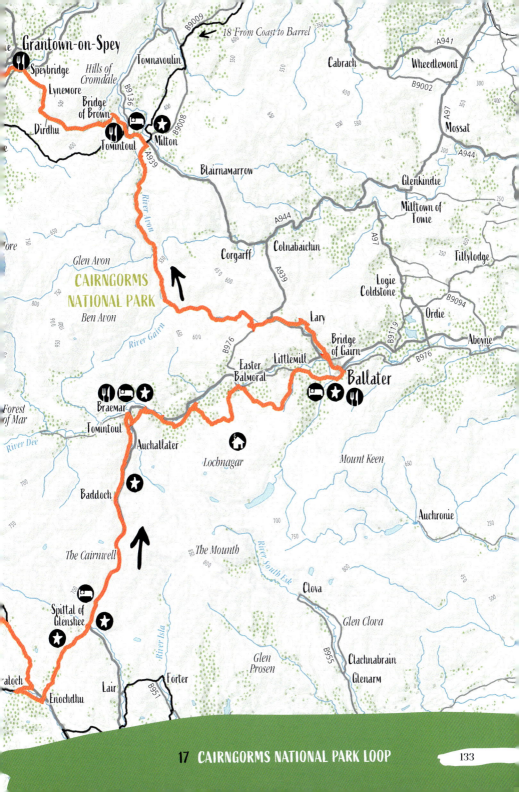

Grantown-on-Spey

Speybridge

Lynemore

Hills of Cromdale

Dirdhu

Bridge of Brown

Tomintoul

Milton

B9136

B9008

B9009

18 From Coast to Barrel

Tomnavoulin

Cabrach

Wheedlemont

B9002

Mossat

A97

A941

A944

Glenkindie

Blairnamarrow

A939

River Avon

Corgarff

Colnabaichin

A944

Milltown of Towie

A97

Glen Avon

CAIRNGORMS NATIONAL PARK

Ben Avon

Logie Coldstone

Ordie

Tillylodge

B9094

River Gairn

B976

Lary

Bridge of Gairn

Ballater

Aboyne

B976

B9119

Easter Balmoral

Littlemill

Forest of Mar

River Dee

Braemar

Tomintoul

Auchallater

Lochnagar

Mount Keen

Auchronie

Baddoch

The Cairnwell

The Mounth

River South Esk

Clova

Glen Clova

Spittal of Glenshee

River Isla

Glen Prosen

B955

Clachnabrain

Glenarm

...aloch

Enochdhu

Lair

Forter

B951

Way and the non-signposted East Highland Way at times. For the curious bikepacker, both provide opportunities to alter the route and explore further. This section of your route travels through Caledonian forest, typical for Strathspey; the landscape with the magnificent Scots pines lining the route is typical for this part of the Cairngorms National Park. The route passes the scenic Uath Lochans, a collection of four small lochs hidden within the ancient pines of Glen Feshie, and continues on the Speyside Way past Insh to Drumguish. Visits to the 18th-century Ruthven Barracks and the village of Kingussie are worth the short detour. Built in 1719 after the 1715 Jacobite rising, Ruthven Barracks are the best-preserved example of four barracks and dominate the countryside here; they give a great insight into a significant period of Scottish history. They are accessible all day and free of charge.

Near Tromie Bridge the route leaves the Speyside Way to continue into Glen Tromie, tracking the river upstream through dense woodland before the glen starts to open up and provide majestic views on to the mountains. What follows is one of the most remote sections of this loop, with no shelter available once you have left the woodland behind. The route slowly climbs on gravel tracks past Loch an t-Seilich to Gaick Lodge. This 19th-century hunting lodge was built to replace an earlier lodge that was destroyed in an avalanche. The route climbs past Loch Bhrodainn to Loch an Dùin, where the well-maintained doubletrack passes the highest point of this section and then turns into a challenging singletrack at the northern end of the loch.

Expect to push your bike for at least some sections along the loch and over the famous Scottish bog once you have reached the southern end. Your effort is rewarded with an amazing gravel track that descends to the A9, from where Sustrans Route 7 is followed into Bruar. Don't let the tarmac fool you, watch out for some rather big potholes along this stretch of long-neglected road. The route continues with fewer potholes, still following Sustrans Route 7, along the B8079 into Blair Atholl. As an alternative, if you want to add a bit more off-road riding, you can follow the Cairngorms Loop instead of the road.

NAVIGATION

The track after Loch an Dùin is very vague and boggy: care is needed in low visibility.

WHEN TO RIDE

Crossing some mountainous terrain, this ride is best ridden between April and November.

WARNINGS

The river crossing after Blair Atholl can be dangerous after heavy rain. An alternative is to continue through Glen Tilt to Braemar instead.

WATER

The big distances between services to resupply on this route are worth noting. From Kincraig, the next stop for food is the House of Bruar, 58 kilometres away. From Blair Atholl, there are no services for 75 kilometres until Braemar. From Ballater to Tomintoul, there are no services on the route for 45 kilometres.

L–R: *Bridge over River Spey near Kincraig; Still Art Installation near Tomintoul; Caledonian pines near Kincraig; Ballochbuie Forest.*

FOOD AND DRINK
· Old Bridge Inn, Aviemore.
  T: 01479 811 137
· Old Post Office Cafe Gallery, Kincraig.
  T: 01540 651 779
· The Bothy Bar, Blair Atholl.
  T: 01796 481 205
· The Bothy, Braemar. T: 01339 741 019
· The Bothy, Ballater. T: 01339 755 191
· Richmond Arms, Tomintoul.
  T: 0151 947 0393
· KJ's Bothy Bakery, Grantown-on-Spey.
  T: 01479 788 011

ACCOMMODATION
· Ravenscraig Guest House, Aviemore.
  T: 01479 810 278
· Blair Castle Caravan Park, Blair
  Atholl. T: 01796 481 263
· The Old Manse of Blair, Blair Atholl.
  T: 01796 483 344
· Gulabin Lodge, Spittal of Glenshee.
  T: 01250 885 255
· Braemar Youth Hostel, Braemar.
  T: 01339 741 659
· Balmoral Arms, Ballater.
  T: 01339 755 413
· Ballater Hostel, Ballater.
  T: 01339 753 752
· The Smugglers Hostel, Tomintoul.
  T: 01807 580 364
· Aviemore Youth Hostel, Aviemore.
  T: 01479 810 345

Blair Atholl is ideal for an overnight stop, with various accommodation options and a craft beer taproom. Entry to the grounds of Blair Castle is included in the campsite fees. The village can also provide a good alternative start or finish, with frequent trains to Aviemore or Perth.

From Blair Atholl, the route follows A Tour of Highland Perthshire for a while, one of the routes described in *Great British Gravel Rides*. The route follows the road past a few houses and on to Loch Moraig, where the public road ends. From here, Beinn a' Ghlò dominates the views: a huge, complex mountain with many ridges, summits and corries. A wide doubletrack eventually turns into singletrack, and shortly afterwards a river crossing will give you at least wet feet; it can be tricky to negotiate after heavy rain. The route continues through dense heather beneath the three Munros of Beinn a' Ghlò, before eventually turning into a gravel track and descending into Glen Loch. You will travel through this wide-open landscape for a while to reach the border of the Cairngorms National Park shortly after Daldhu, where a few houses are the first signs of civilisation. The route continues on a smooth gravel track first and then on a private road through Gleann Fearnach, reversing the route of the Highland Perthshire Drovers Trail (page 113) to Straloch. It's here you'll enter a museum without walls, the Cateran Ecomuseum. The museum provides a great network of gravel and mountain bike itineraries on its website, which can be used to extend the route further. Another good source is the Perthshire Gravel website.

The route passes the historic Kindrogan House on the way to Enochdhu, from where the Cateran Trail is followed for a while. Big, planted forests soon give way to barren hills as you approach the Lunch Hut at Dirnanean, which offers great shelter. From here onwards you'll be travelling in the footsteps of the British royal family as you make your way north. This was

the route taken by Queen Victoria on her way from Dunkeld to
Balmoral in October 1865, riding her Highland pony. You'll get a
good sense of why the Queen stopped for tea on her trek. Once
you reach the top of the trail, which requires some pushing,
a majestic view into Glen Shee is the reward.

The descent is as good as the views, and the church and
standing stone in Spittal of Glenshee are worth a stop. You'll
cross the historic bridge which was constructed by Major
Caulfeild as part of the Blairgowrie to Braemar Military Road,
now largely followed by the A93, part of the SnowRoads scenic
route. The route climbs steadily on the A93 towards the
Cairnwell Pass, Scotland's highest road at 670 metres and the
highest point of this loop. You descend on the A93 first, and
shortly after Newbigging continue on a smaller road on the
opposite side of the river to Braemar, where the route meets
another bikepacking route, the Deeside Trail.

If you are after a more adventurous route, you can follow the
Cateran Trail for a short while out of Spittal of Glenshee, take a
track towards Loch Beanie and follow the route up the Monega
Pass: more information on the Cateran Ecomuseum website.
You'll eventually end up back on the A93 to Braemar.

Braemar, which often records Scotland's coldest tempera-
tures in winter, is home to a thriving outdoor community and
has everything a bikepacker needs: food, an outdoor shop with
cafe, two hostels and, for those who are after luxury, one of
Scotland's finest hotels.

From Braemar, follow the Queen's Drive, a carriage drive
once favoured by Queen Victoria, and then join the A93 to
Invercauld Bridge. A cycle path, currently under construction,
will provide a great alternative to this part of the route. There
are two bridges over the Dee: the new bridge on the A93 is
crossed first, and then the Old Bridge of Dee, which dates back
to 1753 and was built by Major Caulfeild as part of the military

OTHER ROUTES NEARBY

- Highland Perthshire Drovers Trail
  (page 113).
- A Tour of Highland Perthshire –
  www.adventurebooks.com/gbgr
- Speyside Way and Cateran Trail –
  www.scotlandsgreattrails.com
- Badenoch Way –
  www.walkhighlands.co.uk
- East Highland Way –
  www.easthighlandway.com
- Cairngorms Loop –
  www.cairngormsloop.net
- SnowRoads scenic route –
  www.snowroads.com
- Cateran Ecomuseum routes –
  www.cateranecomuseum.co.uk
- Deeside Trail – www.deesidetrail.com
- Deeside Way – www.deesideway.org
- Sustrans National Cycle Network
  routes 7 and 195 – www.sustrans.org.uk
- Perthshire Gravel trails –
  www.perthshiregravel.com

NOTES

- The Cateran Dirt Dash event in
  August follows part of the route.
  www.dirtdash.cc/caterandash
- Thrive Ballater celebrates the local
  bike community. www.thriveballater.com

*L–R: Speyside Way from Aviemore to
Kingussie; Balmoral Castle; gravel path
near Ballater.*

BIKE SHOPS AND HIRE

- Aviemore Bikes, Aviemore (shop, hire).
  T: 01479 810 478
- Backcountry.scot, Aviemore (shop, hire). T: 01479 811 829
- Bothy Bikes, Kingussie (shop, hire).
  T: 01540 667 111
- Cyclehighlands, Ballater (shop).
  T: 01339 755 864
- Bike Station, Ballater (shop, hire).
  T: 01339 754 004
- Ride Scotland, Boat of Garten
  (shop, hire). T: 01479 831 729

VIDEO INSPIRATION

L–R: *Cateran Trail from Enochdhu to Spittal of Glenshee; Glen Gairn.*

road from Perthshire through the mountains to Speyside. What follows from here is a brilliant section through Ballochbuie Forest, one of the largest continuous areas of Caledonian forest in Scotland. You are now on Balmoral Estate, purchased by Prince Albert for Queen Victoria in 1852. On an earlier visit, the surrounding landscape had reminded them of Thuringia, Albert's homeland in Germany and incidentally where the author of this book grew up!

The route continues on a smooth gravel track through the forest, and then climbs towards Ripe Hill, offering great views towards the Lochnagar massif. If you want to add a stay or seek shelter for lunch, Gelder Shiel bothy is just a short detour south once you have crossed the Gelder Burn. The route descends back towards Easter Balmoral (it is possible to make a detour to Prince Albert's Cairn, a pyramid overlooking Balmoral Estate). An alternative from here is to continue on the route of the Deeside Trail, climbing on the track towards Lochnagar and then following the gravel tracks on the western side of Glen Muick to Ballater. Our route passes Royal Lochnagar distillery and then climbs again. From the highest point the route follows a track into a beautiful woodland past an abandoned steading at Bovaglie, and you will pass a few more abandoned houses as you descend into the beautiful Glen Girnock.

The route meets the B976 and crosses the River Dee into

Ballater, which has all the services you might need as well as brilliant bike shops. With trails like Heartbreak Ridge, the village is an ideal base for mountain biking and gravel day trips, and hosts the annual Thrive cycling festival. Ballater is connected to Aberdeen by the Deeside Way, Sustrans Route 195.

Our route once again overlaps with the Deeside Trail and follows the riverside trail out of Ballater. It continues on the eastern side of Glen Gairn to Lary, and after crossing the river on a footbridge joins the A939 to Gairnshiel Bridge and the B976 to Braenaloin. From here, one of the smoothest gravel tracks in Scotland follows the River Gairn through a beautiful valley to Loch Builg, from where the Cairngorms Loop is followed through the rugged landscape of Glen Builg and Glen Avon to the highest village in the Highlands, Tomintoul. While thousands flock to the small village for its famous Whisky Castle shop, and Highland Games, the village is also one of the best places in Scotland to experience dark skies and has an excellent hostel and pub.

The route now follows the A939 to Bridge of Brown, where your climbing legs will be put to a proper test, and then meets the A95 outside of Grantown-on-Spey. KJ's Bothy Bakery is just a short detour from where the route joins the Speyside Way and is worth every metre of extra cycling. KJ, formerly the owner of the Mountain Cafe in Aviemore, turned her bakery in an industrial estate into a great stop for coffee and cake. The route flattens out from here and the Speyside Way is once again followed to Nethy Bridge, passing through an impressive section of Caledonian forest. Boat of Garten is home to one of the finest pump tracks in Scotland and is also one of the stops for the steam trains of the Strathspey Railway. Ride Scotland can help with bike repairs and local riding advice, before the route follows Sustrans Route 7 through another stunning forest to a clearing, which provides superb views on to the highest mountains of the Cairngorms. The route finishes along the Speyside Way into Aviemore.

18 FROM COAST TO BARREL

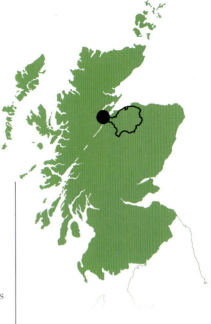

INTRODUCTION

Moray Speyside sits between Inverness and Aberdeen and extends from the Moray coastline south to the Cairngorms National Park. More specifically, this is Whisky Country. Home to more than half of Scotland's whisky distilleries, the region is world-famous. However, it's not just the abundance of distilleries that makes this loop one of the most varied in the book: be prepared to experience a stunning wild coast, breathtaking mountains and one of the most rewarding climbs in the Cairngorms.

THE ROUTE

Starting from Inverness railway station, the route follows Academy Street south and then meets Sustrans Routes 1 and 7, passing the fabulous Velocity Cafe. Follow the Sustrans route on a number of roads to Inshes Roundabout, from where a cycle path takes you to Caulfield Road North. The start of the route is not the most inspiring, but as soon as you get to Old Smithton, you'll leave the Sustrans route and follow a nice singletrack through Culloden Wood. There are a number of trails in this woodland, and our route crosses the railway and meets the Sustrans route again at the Scottish School of Forestry.

The route follows a variety of tracks on to the Culloden Battlefield (£). This is the site of one of the most significant events in Scottish history, the final Jacobite Rising, and one of Scotland's key tourist attractions. If busloads of people are not your thing, you can simply carry on following Sustrans Route 7. The site is cared for by the National Trust for Scotland and has a visitor centre where you can find out more about the last and most harrowing pitched battle fought on British soil.

ROUTE CONDITIONS
· Singletrack: 13%
· Path: 33%
· Cycle path: 7%
· Road: 47%
· Recommended bike: mountain bike

WHEN TO RIDE
This route is best ridden between April and November.

WARNINGS
The alternative on the road from Rothes to Craigellachie is very busy. The route over Burma Road is very exposed.

Elmar Jünemann on the Burma Road.

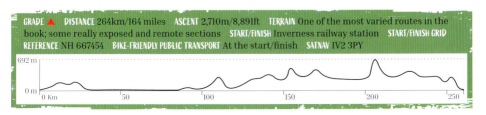

GRADE ▲ DISTANCE 264km/164 miles ASCENT 2,710m/8,891ft TERRAIN One of the most varied routes in the book; some really exposed and remote sections START/FINISH Inverness railway station START/FINISH GRID REFERENCE NH 667454 BIKE-FRIENDLY PUBLIC TRANSPORT At the start/finish SATNAV IV2 3PY

692 m

0 m

0 Km   50   100   150   200   250

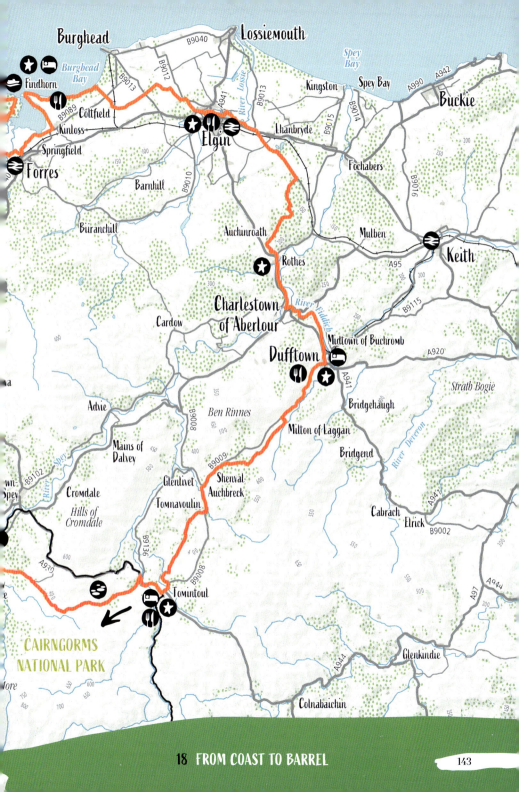

Burghead

Lossiemouth

B9040

Spey Bay

Findhorn

Burghead Bay

B9012

River Lossie

B9013

Kingston

Spey Bay

Buckie

A942

A990

Coltfield

B9089

Kinloss

Elgin

Lhanbryde

B9013

B9015

B9014

Fochabers

Springfield

Forres

Barnhill

B9010

A941

B9016

Buranchill

Auchinroath

Mulben

Keith

Rothes

A95

200

Cardow

Charlestown
of Aberlour

River Fiddich

B9115

Midtown of Buchromb

Dufftown

A920

Strath Bogie

Advie

Ben Rinnes

Bridgehaugh

B9008

River Deveron

Mains of
Dalvey

Milton of Laggan

Bridgend

River Spey

B9102

B9009

Shenval
Auchbreck

Cabrach

Elrick

B9002

Cromdale

Glenlivet

A947

Hills of
Cromdale

Tomnavoulin

B9136

A939

600

B9008

Tomintoul

A941

CAIRNGORMS
NATIONAL PARK

Glenkindie

A944

A97

Colnabaichin

FOOD AND DRINK

- Black Isle Bar & Rooms, Inverness.
  T: 01463 229 920
- Velocity Café & Bicycle Workshop,
  Inverness – www.velocitylove.co.uk
- The Bakery, Inverness. T: 01463 418 918
- Strathnairn Beach Cafe, Nairn –
  www.facebook.com/Strathnairnbeachcafe
- Kimberley Inn, Findhorn.
  T: 01309 690 492
- The Bakehouse, Findhorn.
  T: 01309 691 826
- Batchen Street Coffee, Elgin.
  T: 01343 545 888
- Spice of India, Dufftown.
  T: 01340 820 820
- Richmond Hotel, Tomintoul.
  T: 0151 947 0393
- Nethy House, Nethy Bridge.
  T: 07963 217 793
- The Old Bridge Inn, Aviemore.
  T: 01479 811 137
- Cheese and Tomatin, Aviemore.
  T: 01479 811 565
- The 3 Bridges Café, Tomatin.
  T: 01808 511 709

ACCOMMODATION

- Moyness Guest House, Inverness.
  T: 01463 233 836
- Inverness Youth Hostel, Inverness.
  T: 01463 231 771

L–R: *Distillery near Dufftown; remains
of anti-tank blocks from World War II
near Findhorn; Moray Coast.*

Further along the road you'll soon be able to see the magnificent Culloden Viaduct, which was opened in 1898 in the golden age of railways. This part of the route undulates through the countryside and reaches its highest point in Assich Forest. Near Kirkton of Barevan you leave the Sustrans route and enter the beautiful Cawdor Wood at Achindown Bridge, a single-span Wade-style stone bridge of unknown date. The riding and scenery in this ancient oakwood is fantastic, and you can add in a visit to Cawdor Castle (£), accessible from Cawdor village. There is a small shop in the village for resupplying.

After joining the B9090 for a very short section, a singletrack along the eastern side of the Cawdor Burn is followed through more beautiful woods. The burn eventually flows into the River Nairn and the track continues on its banks and into the town of the same name; this singletrack is fun on a mountain bike. In Nairn, the route meets Sustrans Route 1 for a short section, before continuing through the caravan park into the Culbin Sands Nature Reserve. Following the Sustrans route would provide an alternative, but the paths and singletracks along this stunning part of the Moray Coast are one of the highlights of this route. At low tide you can watch out for bar-tailed godwits, oystercatchers and knots feeding along the shoreline, while high tide brings sea ducks close to the sand dunes. You might spot seals here too. There is an abundance of trails in Culbin Forest if you want to extend the route.

Our route circumnavigates the vast Findhorn Bay, but North 58° Sea Adventures (*www.north58.co.uk*) also runs a seasonal water taxi to Findhorn, which saves a good 15 kilometres of riding. After exiting Culbin Forest you follow Sustrans Route 1 to Kinloss on quiet roads, from where the road into Findhorn takes you past the former military base and the pioneering Findhorn Ecovillage. Findhorn has a great hostel, a pub and there is a shop for basic supplies. Even if the Bakehouse appears to be closed in the early morning, you can still buy its tasty bread at the back door (just knock).

What follows after Findhorn is a stunning section along the beautiful and quiet Moray Coast. Continuing on the Moray Coast Trail, you will pass the Findhorn Heritage Centre, including an icehouse with its underground chambers built in the mid 19th century to store ice for packing the salmon en route to London. At low tide you can easily ride along the beach, or follow the signposted route at high tide (or if you have narrower tyres). Remains of anti-tank blocks from World War II line the coast and are still in good condition, and the colourful beach huts make for great photos. At a car park the route leaves the Moray Coast Trail and meets the Sustrans route again after three kilometres. This pretty flat stretch soon comes to an end as the route climbs through Quarrelwood into Elgin.

Elgin is a former cathedral city and the administrative centre for Moray. It has plenty of eateries and there's a well-stocked bike shop. The remains of the cathedral passed on your way out of town are impressive, and a nice cycle path follows the River Lossie to Barmuckity. The route continues on the cycle path alongside the busy A96 with a very short section on the road, before the B9103 is followed to Teindland Wood. The gravel track through this extensive woodland climbs steadily at first and is much more fun than the road. After descending towards Glen of Rothes you will pass the first distillery of the route, Speyburn, on the way into Rothes, which welcomes you to Scotland's whisky country. From here onwards you could spend days on the route if you wanted to visit each distillery. The route follows the Rothes Way, which is, at the time of writing, not yet finished. The alternative is to follow the road, but you will very soon figure out why the local community is working on establishing an alternative to the super-busy main road.

From Craigellachie the route follows the Speyside Way into Dufftown. The 'Malt Whisky Capital of the World', Dufftown is home to several active distilleries – including Balvenie, Dufftown, Glendullan, Glenfiddich, Kininvie and Mortlach – and produces more whisky than any other town in Scotland.

- Black Isle Bar & Rooms, Inverness. T: 01463 229 920
- The Findhorn Village Centre & Hostel, Findhorn. T: 01309 692 339
- Dufftown Square Apartment, Dufftown (search online).
- The Smugglers Hostel, Tomintoul. T: 01807 580 364
- The Lazy Duck, Nethy Bridge. T: 07846 291 154
- Aviemore Youth Hostel, Aviemore. T: 01479 810 345
- Ravenscraig Guest House, Aviemore. T: 01479 810 278

OTHER ROUTES NEARBY

- Cairngorms National Park Loop (page 131), A Scottish Hostelling Adventure (page 151) and An Alternative North Coast 500 (page 161).
- North Coast 500 – page 168 and www.northcoast500.com
- Sustrans National Cycle Network routes 1 and 7 – www.sustrans.org.uk
- The Moray Coast Trail – www.morayways.org.uk
- Speyside Way – www.speysideway.org
- SnowRoads scenic route – www.snowroads.com
- Cairngorms Loop – www.cairngormsloop.net
- Caledonia Way (parts are Sustrans Route 78) – www.visitscotland.com

BIKE SHOPS AND HIRE

· Ticket to Ride, Inverness (hire).
  T: 01463 419 160
· Velocity Café & Bicycle Workshop,
  Inverness (shop) –
  www.velocitylove.co.uk
· Bikes of Inverness, Inverness (shop).
  T: 01463 225 965
· Highland Bikes, Inverness (shop).
  T: 01463 234 789
· Alpine Bikes @ Tiso, Inverness (shop).
  T: 01463 729 171
· Highland Bikes, Elgin (shop).
  T: 01343 543 846
· Ride Scotland, Boat of Garten
  (shop, hire). T: 01479 831 729
· Aviemore Bikes, Aviemore (shop, hire).
  T: 01479 810 478
· Alpine Bikes @ Tiso, Aviemore
  (shop, hire). T: 01479 788 840
· Backcountry.Scot, Aviemore
  (shop, hire). T: 01479 811 829

L–R: *Elgin Cathedral; woodland near Cawdor; Elmar Jünemann and Christian Urbanski on the ascent to the Mains of Quirn.*

If you are after a tasting or tour at a distillery, you'll be hard pushed to find a better place. Navigation in Dufftown is easy as all four main roads meet at the Dufftown clock tower, which was originally used as a prison. There are a few restaurants and shops in the small town, but choices are limited. On the way into town you pass the terminus of the Keith and Dufftown Railway, which still services the 18-kilometre link between Dufftown and the historic town of Keith on the Malt Whisky Trail. Balvenie Castle, after which the single malt is named, is a short detour off the route.

A small path right next to the B9009 takes you out of Dufftown to Glenrinnes Lodge, from where the route continues along the road to Milton of Laggan. The surroundings here are different, with the peaks of Little Conval, Meikle Conval and Ben Rinnes dominating the landscape. While the route travels mostly through low-lying pastoral landscapes, this section through Glen Rinnes takes you gradually into the more rugged beauty of the Cairngorms National Park. The route follows a small country road and then a gravel track through a forest to Lagavaich, and continues on the B9009 into Glenlivet. At a junction the route travels south to Tomnavoulin, home to another distillery. From here, an at first gradual and then very steep climb takes you first on to open moorland and then through a forest on the Speyside Way (Tomintoul Spur) to Tomintoul. This is where the route overlaps with the Cairngorms National Park Loop (page 131), which provides an alternative (and less rugged) route to Aviemore.

The small, planned village of Tomintoul is not only the highest village in the Highlands, but also the only designated dark sky park in this part of Scotland. Surely you'll be whiskied out by now, although it is hard not to visit the Whisky Castle shop which has by far the largest selection of whiskies you could find. As you are probably unlikely to want to carry a bottle with you, you can have your favourite dram shipped home as well.

The local hotel is great for food.

From Tomintoul, the route follows the SnowRoads scenic route. While cycling up the path to the art installation shortly after the village on the right adds a few more metres of climbing to an already hilly route, both the views and the sculpture are worthwhile. At Kylnadrochit Lodge the route follows the Cairngorms Loop on a beautiful gravel track. But don't be fooled by either scenery or maps because as soon as you descend to Glen Brown you must mentally prepare yourself for wet feet: as the doubletrack meanders through this beautiful valley, it fords the river at least seven times in one kilometre. After leaving the river and its crossings behind, you'll climb on a nice smooth gravel track to the head of the glen at Letteraitten. The downhill from here to Dorback Lodge is much drier and very enjoyable, and from the former shooting lodge you follow roads all the way into Nethy Bridge, home to one of Scotland's cosiest hostels.

From here the route passes through Caledonian forest on the Speyside Way to Boat of Garten, and onwards to the outskirts of Aviemore. You can enjoy very smooth gravel tracks and great views on to some of the highest mountains in Scotland. This route follows paths and quiet roads into Aviemore, but both signposted options, the Speyside Way and Sustrans Route 7, are good options into the town centre as well. Aviemore is by far the busiest town in the Cairngorms National Park and offers lots of choice for accommodation and eating out; be prepared to book ahead at any time of year to avoid disappointment.

From Aviemore, the B9152 takes you to Lynwilg Farm where you cross the A9 to the start of the Burma Road, one of Scotland's classic mountain bike climbs. After 460 metres of climbing you can enjoy amazing views across the mountains of the Cairngorms in all directions, before being rewarded with a fast downhill to the River Dulnain. This route is very exposed, but as soon as you reach Caggan you can enjoy the shelter and beauty of more Caledonian forest.

At Sluggan the route joins Sustrans Route 7 again, passing a single-arch bridge which replaced an earlier bridge built by George Wade as part of a military road. The old bridge was washed away in the floods of 1829, and the present one was put up some time after After leaving the Sustrans route, General Wade's Military Road is followed to Slochd, from where you are back on cycle paths and quiet roads to Tomatin, home to an excellent community cafe with bike facilities.

Continue on to Daviot, and from here follow the military road again, mostly on tracks, to the outskirts of Inverness. A mixture of cycle paths and roads leads back to the finish at Inverness railway station. From Inverness, there are plenty of opportunities to extend the adventure, for example by using the An Alternative North Coast 500 (page 161) or A Scottish Hostelling Adventure (page 151) routes, the Caledonia Way or the North Coast 500 (page 168).

SPOTLIGHT ROSS O'REILLY

PRODUCING BESPOKE BIKEPACKING BAGS MADE IN SCOTLAND

@straightcutdesign

Ross designs and manufactures custom and bespoke bike storage solutions at his studio in Edinburgh. After studying product design, he started his own business, Straight Cut® Design.

'I have been racing and riding since I was young. Biking has always been part of me as a person. I got introduced to bikepacking before I started anything on a professional level business wise. At first it was a love–hate relationship. I remember a really cold winter and getting taken to a bothy on the bike, super unprepared and borrowing kit. But I was hooked on the freedom to go wherever you want and I loved it. Each trip still offers me inspiration for

the company, from product creation to the continued development of dealing with Scottish conditions: really rough and unforgiving.

'People come for the quality. It's different from what other people can offer. But most people don't know it's me emailing you, talking to you, shipping orders and making the bags. A lot of people don't know that. They think it's a much bigger enterprise. And that's not to say it won't be. For some people, once they find that out, it gives them perhaps more brand loyalty. Because they realise I've poured everything into it for them.

'I would say currently my business is sustainable: I design products that are made

THE ROUTE

The Badger Divide
(*www.instagram.com/ thebadgerdivide*) is a popular 337-kilometre/209-mile bike-packing route from Inverness to Glasgow, devised and mapped by Stu Allen.

Ross's highlights on the route: *'I typically ride south to north, so towards Inverness. I think it's the more enjoyable way. It's a great route. I love it because it's quite technical in a lot of areas and I prefer riding on really rough, steep terrain, loaded or unloaded. My favourite place is a camp spot, and it's just unreal. As you pass into Ardverikie Estate, you go over the main road and up to the double lochans. At that first lochan there's a small bit about halfway along on your right-hand side, a little bit of tree outcrop right on the lochan. Me and my mate camped right on the edge there, and it was just the best. So quiet, no one else was there, and it was crystal clear in the morning.'*

to endure. If you can create a product with a longer lifespan and which is repairable, that's going to be better than buying something that is more sustainable but replaces something that isn't. The first customer bag is probably just about six years old. It has only been repaired once, but it had two zipper replacements and it's still good.

'In bikepacking there has been a shift – more and more people are starting to go on adventures. In Edinburgh and further afield there are great groups that do specifically that, and it has become just a lot more accessible as a result. I also think it has a lot to do with lockdown. There has been a big shift in terms of people's priorities. People realised they didn't want to sit behind a desk all day. It doesn't take much to get into cycling and have a good time.'

VIDEO INSPIRATION

L–R: Ardverikie Estate © Ross O'Reilly; Straight Cut® Design bags and studio in Edinburgh; Ross cycling on the streets of Edinburgh © Ross O'Reilly.

19 A SCOTTISH HOSTELLING ADVENTURE

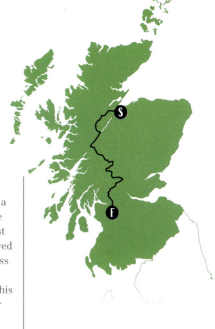

INTRODUCTION

Cycling and hostelling is a wonderful combination that has proven successful and enjoyable for many years. Scouted on a 1970s Claud Butler, this route was created as a homage to the Rough-Stuff Fellowship – the many women and men who first took their bikes off-road in the mid-1950s and who often stayed in hostels overnight. Running from the east coast at Inverness to the west coast at Glasgow, and with an abundance of nice hostels along the way for those who want to take less stuff, this itinerary can be used as an alternative to the popular Badger Divide or as a return journey.

THE ROUTE

The adventure starts at Inverness railway station and follows Sustrans Route 1 north along the banks of the River Ness out of the city. As you approach the Kessock Bridge, the route leaves the Sustrans route and continues around the Caledonian Stadium to the eastbound cycle lane and continues over the bridge. (If the westbound cycle lane is open, the approach to and from the bridge is a little different.) Sustrans Route 1 is followed until Charleston, and from here a quiet road takes you along the shore of the Beauly Firth to Milton of Redcastle. After a short stint on the A832 you'll hit the first of many gravel tracks taking you through farmland, before joining the A862 to Beauly. You'll pass the railway station, which is also the start of Jenny's coast-to-coast route from *Great British Gravel Rides*. In Beauly, the route also connects with the North Coast 500 (page 168), the popular touring route around Northern Scotland.

From Beauly you continue on the A862 and A831 for a short while, before a quieter road is followed to Fanellan, the first

ROUTE CONDITIONS

· Singletrack: 6%
· Path: 40%
· Cycle path: 6%
· Road: 48%
· Recommended bike: gravel bike

On the Road to the Isles from Corrour to Rannoch.

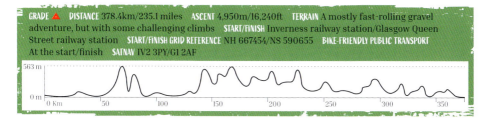

GRADE ▲   DISTANCE 378.4km/235.1 miles   ASCENT 4,950m/16,240ft   TERRAIN A mostly fast-rolling gravel adventure, but with some challenging climbs   START/FINISH Inverness railway station/Glasgow Queen Street railway station   START/FINISH GRID REFERENCE NH 667454/NS 590655   BIKE-FRIENDLY PUBLIC TRANSPORT At the start/finish   SATNAV IV2 3PY/G1 2AF

563 m

0 m

0 Km   50   100   150   200   250   300   350

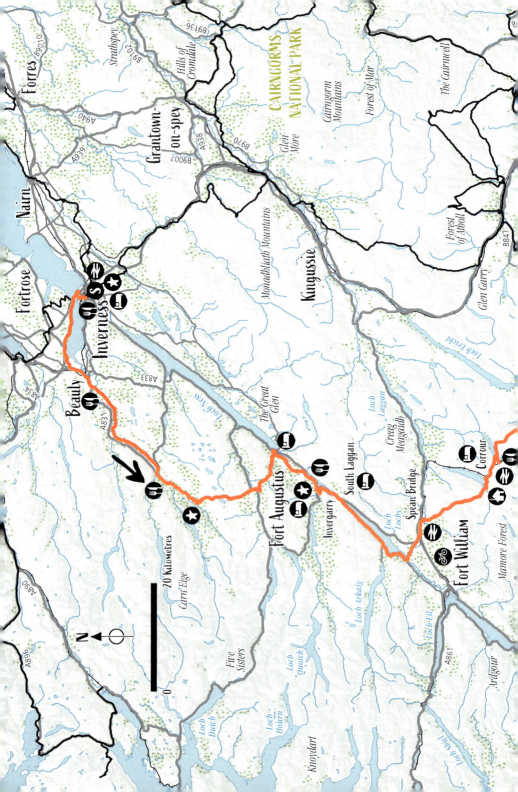

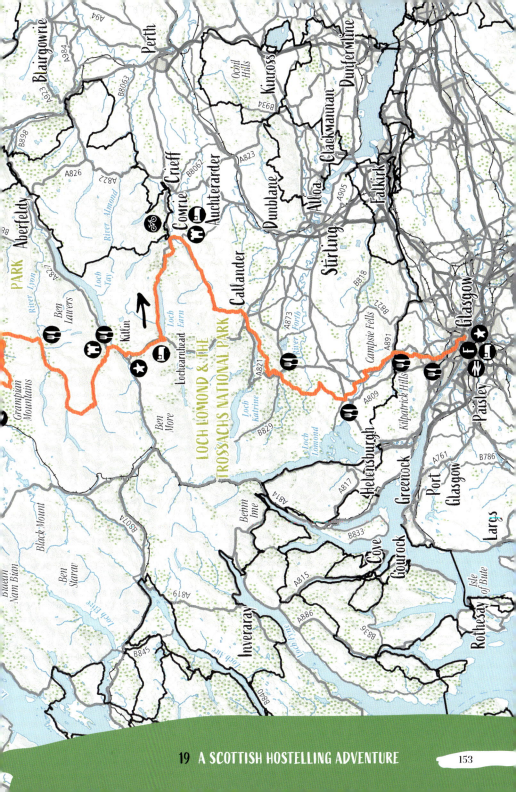

noticeable climb on the route. The route continues on this road through a beautiful valley, following the River Beauly. From the confluence of the rivers Beauly and Glass near Struy the route continues through the beautiful Strathglass to Cannich. If you stop, look out for the teapot collection at Cannich Stores and Post Office. From Cannich you follow the route of the Highland Trail 550 (page 122) and pass Tomich, a planned village with properties that were originally created to serve Guisachan House, whose ruins you can spot shortly afterwards from the gravel track that leads to Plodda Falls. This estate is where the golden retriever was first bred by Sir Dudley Marjoribanks (Baron Tweedmouth). His influence on the landscape is clearly visible at Plodda Falls, where an almost-vertical cascade drops into the Abhainn Deabhag beneath the many Douglas firs, larch, grand fir and redwoods which he had planted.

The route follows a steep gravel trail out of Guisachan Forest, tracking the pylons of the Beauly to Denny power line, and reaches its highest point at a loch from where there are stunning views on to the mountains of Kintail. The route continues on this wide gravel track and descends into Glen Moriston, where it meets the Old Military Road. Instead of continuing on the military road, you can follow the service track for the pylons to rejoin the main route at Inchnacardoch Forest. While most of the riding is on wide tracks, the descent into Fort Augustus is more technical. In Fort Augustus, the route meets the Caledonia Way, and also the Badger Divide (page 148), another popular bikepacking route from Inverness to Glasgow.

The next section alongside the Caledonian Canal from Fort Augustus to Aberchalder offers relaxed riding on a wide towpath with fabulous views of the nearby mountains. After crossing the Aberchalder Swing Bridge the route passes the Bridge of Oich, an innovative suspension bridge designed by a brewer-turned-engineer James Dredge in 1854. The route continues on the Great Glen Way, one of Scotland's Great Trails, through a forest to Invergarry. If you are riding the route in three days, as I did, then Saddle Mountain Hostel in Invergarry is an excellent overnight option to shelter from the midges.

From Invergarry, the route follows gravel tracks above

WHEN TO RIDE
This route is at its best between April and November.

WARNINGS
The section between Spean Bridge and Corrour Station is not suitable for gravel bikes, and the train is the better option. In addition, be mindful that there are no services until the Glenlyon Tearoom, and, if this is closed, until Killin.

NOTES
Find out more about the Rough-Stuff Fellowship on their website or in the excellent two books that portray their journeys.
www.rsf.org.uk

L–R: Guisachan House; rider on the old coffin road to Killin during GBDURO; Loch Laidon near Rannoch; Saddle Mountain Hostel; Cultybraggan Camp.

FOOD AND DRINK

- The Bakery, Inverness.
  T: 01463 418 918
- Velocity Café & Bicycle Workshop,
  Inverness – www.velocitylove.co.uk
- Black Isle Bar & Rooms, Inverness.
  T: 01463 229 920
- Corner on the Square, Beauly.
  T: 01463 783 000
- Bog Cotton Café, Cannich.
  T: 07946 566 174
- Invergarry Hotel, Invergarry.
  T: 01809 501 206
- Corrour Station House, Corrour.
  T: 01397 732 236
- Glenlyon Tearoom, Bridge of Balgie.
  T: 01887 866 324
- The Falls Of Dochart Inn, Killin.
  T: 01567 820 770
- Macgregors, Aberfoyle.
  T: 01877 389 376
- Drymen Bakery & Deli, Drymen.
  T: 01360 660 070
- Coffee at The Wilsons, Blanefield.
  T: 07752 203 873
- Finsbay, Milngavie. T: 0141 956 6016

Loch Oich, and meets the Caledonia Way again at North Laggan. The next section of the Caledonian Canal, connecting Loch Oich and Loch Lochy, is known as Laggan Avenue and it is one of the best places to canoe in Scotland. Lined by massive trees, it is particularly stunning in autumn. The route continues on gravel tracks along the western shore of Loch Lochy on the Caledonia Way, and takes a small detour from the Sustrans route to follow the Great Glen Way before Gairlochy. Here you leave the signposted route on the B8004, a singletrack road that leads to the Commando Memorial near Spean Bridge. Spean Bridge is served by the West Highland Railway Line and the Caledonian Sleeper.

To avoid a long hike-a-bike section after Lairig Leacach bothy, the next part of the route from Spean Bridge to Corrour Station is best done by train. If you cycle, follow the route of the East Highland Way south of the River Spean to Corriechoile and the start of a long and steep climb on a landrover track along the Allt Leachdach. Shortly before the bothy, the track starts descending into the Lairig Leacach and continues on a technical singletrack all the way to Creaguaineach Lodge on the shore of Loch Treig. While more rideable downhill than uphill, this is a hike-a-bike section for most. From the shores of the loch a good gravel track climbs towards Loch Ossian. If taking the train, you start again at Corrour Station, Britain's highest railway station and a good place to stop for food (the station house is usually open from the end of March to October). The hostel at Loch Ossian is basic, but great if you want to enjoy the surroundings for longer while avoiding the midges.

The scenery around the loch is stunning. The route rejoins the Badger Divide here to continue past the ruins of the Old Corrour Lodge towards Loch Rannoch. Once Scotland's highest shooting lodge, it was replaced by a more easily accessible lodge

at the east end of Loch Ossian in 1896 following the opening of the railway in 1894. This route, a former drove road, is also known as the Road to the Isles and reaches the B846, the first public road for a while, at the shores of Loch Eigheach. Rannoch railway station is a bit further to the west, while you continue on tarmac for a while to Bridge of Gaur on the western edge of Loch Rannoch. This area was formerly part of the native Caledonian forest that stretched across much of Northern Scotland. While the native woodlands are now largely absent from much of the area and Loch Rannoch is surrounded by commercial forestry and open hillsides, a small area of the native forest remains at the Black Wood of Rannoch, through which the route travels after skirting around Leagag on gravel tracks.

At the edge of the forest you continue on the Kirk Road through the Lairig Ghallabhaich into Glen Lyon, Scotland's longest enclosed glen. The scenery and views from the highest point are once again stunning, and the downhill to Innerwick is highly enjoyable. Here the route joins a minor road into the remote glen to Bridge of Balgie. As food stops are rare on this part of the route, please check the opening times of the Glenlyon tearoom in advance; it's a popular stop for cyclists. From here the public road is followed to Loch Lyon, where the route joins an old coffin road to Killin. The climb from the loch is steep, and the road turns into a gravel track at times, before descending into the remote Glen Lochay. From Kenknock Farm the gravel track turns into a public road again and continues on the bank of the River Lochay to meet the A827 just before Killin. This section of the route mostly overlaps with the Great North Trail and GB Divide routes, but passes the Moirlanich Longhouse shortly before the village. This beautifully conserved cottage, unchanged since it was last inhabited in 1968, is a unique chance to get an insight into rural family life in 19th-century Scotland.

ACCOMMODATION

- Black Isle Hostel, Inverness.
  T: 01463 233 933
- Morag's Lodge, Fort Augustus.
  T: 01320 366 289
- Saddle Mountain Hostel, Invergarry.
  T: 01809 501 412
- Great Glen Hostel, South Laggan.
  T: 01809 501 430
- Loch Ossian Youth Hostel.
  T: 01397 732 207
- Tomrannoch Hostel, Lochearnhead.
  T: 01567 830 219
- Comrie Croft, Comrie. T: 01764 670 140
- Callander Hostel, Callander.
  T: 01877 330 141
- Glasgow Youth Hostel, Glasgow.
  T: 0141 332 3004

L–R: *Road to the Isles from Corrour to Rannoch; climbing towards Glen Lyon.*

L–R: Laggan Avenue; cycle path on the former railway line near Comrie; railway viaduct in Glen Ogle.

As the River Dochart approaches Killin, its bed broadens out and at the same time its gradient steepens. The result is one of the most spectacular waterfalls in Scotland, the Falls of Dochart, which you pass shortly before the route climbs on Sustrans Route 7 through a woodland to the top of Glen Ogle. From here it is mostly downhill to Lochearnhead on the route of the former Callander and Oban Railway, passing the impressive Glen Ogle viaduct along the way. The route leaves the Sustrans route and continues on the A85 into Lochearnhead. Tomrannoch Hostel, just off the main road, is a good option for the second night of a three-day itinerary.

The route follows a track and joins the line of the former Lochearnhead, St Fillans and Comrie Railway. Sections of the route have already been converted into a cycle path, with the long-term aim being to complete the whole route; this is a great alternative to the busy A85. Pass St Fillians and continue through the River Earn National Scenic Area to Comrie. The village is positioned right on the Highland Boundary Fault, which explains why it experiences more earth tremors than anywhere else in Britain; the small Earthquake House is only a short detour off the route and contains old and modern seismological instruments. The Highland Perthshire Drovers Trail (page 113) gives the option to extend your trip from Comrie.

You follow the B827 out of Comrie and Cultybraggan Camp (£) is next, the only remaining World War II prisoner of war camp in Scotland and now a museum. From here, a small public road climbs steadily into Glen Artney. While there is a gravel track on the northern side of the River Artney, this can often be very boggy so the road is the better alternative. Where the road ends, a great gravel track climbs steeply before a fantastic descent takes you into Callander.

Here the route joins Sustrans Route 7 along the shores of Loch

Venachar to Invertrossachs, and then continues to Loch Drunkie; this is part of the Gravelfoyle route from *Great British Gravel Rides*. The route joins the Sustrans route again to descend into Aberfoyle, home to the first waymarked gravel trails in Scotland. You follow the signed Faerie Loop out of the village; this is also the route of the Rob Roy Way. On your way you pass an aqueduct of the Glasgow Corporation Water Works scheme, which supplied the city with fresh drinking water from Loch Katrine by gravity. The route diverts from the Rob Roy Way before the road is met, where you continue on Sustrans Route 7 into Drymen, a village which was once a popular stopping place for cattle drovers and nowadays is a gateway for visitors to Loch Lomond. Drymen is also a popular stop on the West Highland Way.

From Drymen you continue on Sustrans Route 7 to Killearn, where the route joins the Pipe Track, another heritage path. This track between Killearn and Blanefield was part of the construction of the Glasgow Corporation Water Works scheme. The pipes of the scheme are mostly hidden, but you can spot many other structures along the route, such as masonry aqueduct bridges which cross the many burns flowing from the slopes to the east, as well as byewashes, shafts, sinks, a valve house and even gates and stiles which date from the time of the track's construction. The riding here is fantastic, with stunning views of the surrounding countryside and impressive woodlands. In Blanefield, the route meets the John Muir Way (page 63), a great extension to this route, before following small country roads into Mugdock Country Park and on to Milngavie, the start of the West Highland Way. From here, the route follows the Bears Way, the Kelvin Walkway, Sustrans Route 756 and roads to the finish at Glasgow Queen Street railway station.

BIKE SHOPS AND HIRE

- Ticket to Ride, Inverness (hire).
  T: 01463 419 160
- Bikes of Inverness, Inverness (shop).
  T: 01463 225 965
- Highland Bikes, Inverness (shop).
  T: 01463 234 789
- Alpine Bikes @ Tiso, Inverness (shop).
  T: 01463 729 171
- Orange Fox Bikes, Muir of Ord (shop).
  T: 01463 870 346
- Girvans Hardware, Fort Augustus (shop, hire). T: 01320 366 864
- Comrie Croft Bikes, Comrie (shop, hire).
  T: 01764 670 140
- Wheels Cycling Centre, Callander (hire). T: 01877 331 100
- Aberfoyle Bike Hire & Cafe (shop, hire). T: 01877 382 023
- Country Cycles, Killearn (shop).
  T: 01360 550 372
- Gear Bikes, Glasgow (shop, hire).
  T: 0141 339 1179
- Dales Cycles, Glasgow (shop).
  T: 0141 332 2705

VIDEO INSPIRATION

20 AN ALTERNATIVE NORTH COAST 500

INTRODUCTION

The world-renowned North Coast 500 (page 168) takes in over 500 miles of stunning coastal scenery in the far north of Scotland, following the main roads along the coastal edges of the Northern Highlands and visiting the regions of Wester Ross, Sutherland, Caithness, Easter Ross, the Black Isle and Inverness-shire. Based on the obvious time constraints that make it difficult for people to cycle the whole NC500, this new and shorter itinerary can be ridden in less time and with less traffic, while still featuring iconic places along the NC500 route such as Bealach na Bà, the third highest road in Scotland.

THE ROUTE

The route starts on the shore of Loch Carron at Strathcarron railway station; there's a small hotel and shop near the station. From here you follow the route of the Highland Trail 550 (page 122) in reverse for a short section on the A890 and then continue on the A896 and the NC500 route to Lochcarron, a small village with a cafe and shop. The road climbs out of Lochcarron and descends to Loch Kishorn where there are stunning views. From Tornapress you'll start the climb up the Bealach na Bà, the third highest road in Scotland. This section of the route is an out-and-back journey, but you can also continue on the NC500 to Applecross and cycle on the coastal road to Shieldaig. You climb on a winding singletrack road through the mountains of the Applecross peninsula to the highest point of the route. This historic mountain pass was engineered similarly to roads through the great mountain passes in the Alps with very tight hairpin bends. Starting from near sea level it rises to 626 metres in 9.1 kilometres, reaching 20 per cent at its steepest gradient.

ROUTE CONDITIONS
- Singletrack: 1%
- Path: 12%
- Cycle path: 4%
- Road: 83%
- Recommended bike: gravel bike

Looking towards the mountains of Torridon near Shieldaig.

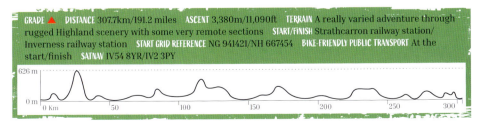

GRADE ▲ **DISTANCE** 307.7km/191.2 miles **ASCENT** 3,380m/11,090ft **TERRAIN** A really varied adventure through rugged Highland scenery with some very remote sections **START/FINISH** Strathcarron railway station/ Inverness railway station **START GRID REFERENCE** NG 941421/NH 667454 **BIKE-FRIENDLY PUBLIC TRANSPORT** At the start/finish **SATNAV** IV54 8YR/IV2 3PY

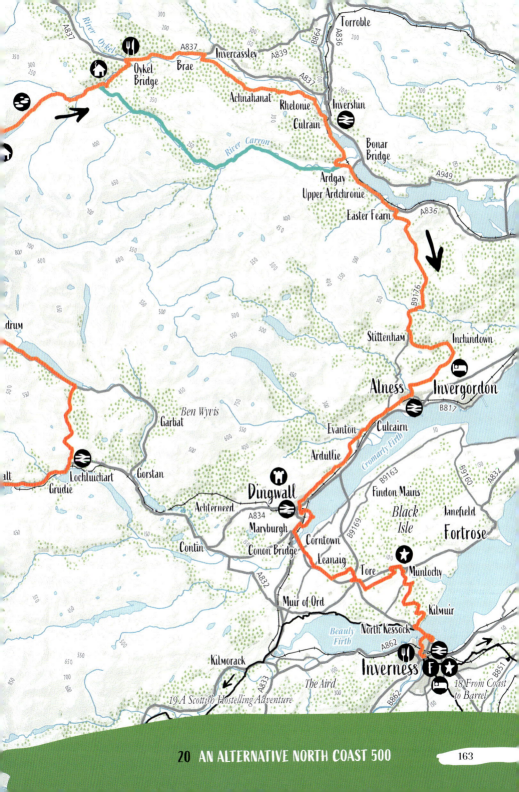

Returning on the same route, you continue north on the A896, which turns into a singletrack road, through the beautiful scenery of Glenshieldaig Forest to Loch Dughaill and on to Shieldaig, a picturesque village on the shore of Loch Shieldaig with largely white-washed cottages. Clearly visible from the shore and covered almost entirely with Caledonian pine trees, the scenic Shieldaig Island has a thriving bird population and provides a beautiful setting for a sunset. You don't have to go far until the next photo opportunity, as you climb on a small road out of the village and rejoin the A896. To the left there are amazing views across Upper Loch Torridon. At Balgy you join a gravel track along the shore and through a nice woodland with Scots pines. The route rejoins the NC500 route at Torridon Hotel and continues on the road through Glen Torridon. You'll likely encounter not only other human beings, but also deer in the car parks on the road here. The scenery is dominated by the imposing ridge of Liathach, which stands between Loch Torridon and the neighbouring mountain of Beinn Eighe. At Loch Clair the route meets the Highland Trail 550 to continue into Kinlochewe. Loch Maree, Scotland's fourth largest freshwater loch, is a worthwhile detour.

At Kinlochewe the route leaves the NC500 and steadily climbs through Glen Docherty and past Loch a' Chroisg to Achnasheen. From here the scenery becomes more open, following the River Bran through Strath Bran. If the traffic on this route is too much for your liking, you can substitute this section by getting a train from Achnasheen to Lochluichart instead. At Loch Luichart the route leaves the road and climbs steeply on a gravel track into Corriemoillie Forest. Close to the Lochluichart wind farm you reach the highest point of this section, with a stunning descent through the wind farm as reward. The views from here across Corriemoillie Forest and Kinlochluichart and Aultchonier Forest are great on a clear day. The route meets the A835 at Loch Glascarnoch. If you want to extend the route, you can join the Great North Trail, GB Divide and Highland Trail 550 routes by turning right on the road towards Garve.

From here, you continue north on the A835 to the spectacular Corrieshalloch Gorge, carved by glacial meltwater over

WHEN TO RIDE
With some very remote sections, this route is best ridden between April and November.

WARNINGS
Some of the road sections are busy due to the popularity of the NC500 route. The section between Ullapool and Oykel Bridge has an abundance of fords and a river crossing that can be tricky after heavy rain. Make sure to have sufficient supplies as this will take longer than expected.

FOOD AND DRINK
· Strathcarron Hotel, Strathcarron.
  T: 01520 722 277
· Bealach Café & Gallery, Tornapress.
  T: 01520 733 436
· Kinlochewe Service Station,
  Kinlochewe. T: 01445 760 277
· The Midge Bite Cafe, Achnasheen.
  T: 01445 720 222
· Oykel Bridge Hotel, Oykel Bridge.
  T: 01549 441 218
· The Bakery, Inverness. T: 01463 418 918
· Black Isle Bar & Rooms, Inverness.
  T: 01463 229 920
· Velocity Café & Bicycle Workshop,
  Inverness – www.velocitylove.co.uk

L.–R: Bealach na Bà; gravel track through a nice woodland near Balgy; bridge over the Ullapool River; Glen Docherty.

ACCOMMODATION
- Tigh an Eilean, Shieldaig.
  T: 01520 755 251
- Ullapool Youth Hostel, Ullapool.
  T: 01854 612 254
- Harbour House, Ullapool.
  T: 01854 612 222
- White Rose Tower, Invergordon
  (detour). T: 01862 842 704
- Moyness Guest House, Inverness.
  T: 01463 233 836
- Inverness Youth Hostel, Inverness.
  T: 01463 231 771
- Black Isle Bar & Rooms, Inverness.
  T: 01463 229 920

OTHER ROUTES NEARBY
- From Coast to Barrel (page 141)
  and A Scottish Hostelling Adventure
  (page 151).
- North Coast 500 – page 168 and
  www.northcoast500.com
- Highland Trail 550 – page 122 and
  www.highlandtrail550.weebly.com
- Badger Divide – page 148 and
  www.instagram.com/thebadgerdivide
- Great North Trail – www.cyclinguk.org
- GB Divide – www.gbdivide.net
- Caledonia Way (parts are Sustrans
  Route 78) – www.visitscotland.com
- Sustrans National Cycle Network
  Route 1 – www.sustrans.org.uk

10,000 years ago. The route joins the NC500 again, and after another section on the main road through Lael Forest a great gravel track takes you through Strath More before the road is rejoined into Ullapool.

The next section of the route starts with an iconic coast-to-coast journey eastbound from Ullapool. There are a few different ways to leave town; this route takes you out on a tarmac road first, and then follows a well-graded track alongside Ullapool River past a working quarry. The route soon joins the Highland Trail 550 again in reverse and continues along the shores of Loch Achall and into Glen Achall. Enjoy superb Highland scenery before the route climbs steeply once past East Rhidorroch Lodge. Once again you'll be rewarded with fine views, before a bothy on the shore of Loch an Daimh provides the perfect lunch stop. Prepare to get your feet wet – there are a number of fords to cross on this stretch and some are deeper and more technical than others. These are just the practice runs for the crossing of the Abhainn Poiblidh at a sheepfold – now this can be *deep*. From here, a well-graded gravel track takes you to another bothy and on to Oykel Bridge.

You now have two options: either follow the route as described here, or follow the Highland Trail 550 to Croick and rejoin the route at Ardgay. If you follow the route as mapped here, continue on the A837 and then cross the river at Inveroykel to proceed on a very scenic and quiet road to Culrain. Culrain has a train station, so the next part of the route can be done by bike or train. From Culrain, follow Sustrans Route 1 south to Ardgay, and on to Fearn. At the distinctive AA sentry box the route follows the B9176 to the viewpoint on Cadha Mor where you'll be rewarded with great views across

Struie Hill and the Dornoch Firth. The route continues through sheer endless woodlands to Strathy from where it follows a gravel track through the woodland to rejoin the road after Easter Achnacloich. Continue on Sustrans Route 1 into Alness.

A nice cycle path runs parallel to the main road to Evanton, and from here the route continues on Sustrans Route 1 into Dingwall. Very little remains of it today, but Dingwall Castle was once the biggest castle north of Stirling, while parts of Tulloch Castle on the edge of town may date back to the 12th century. You follow a path along the coast around a rifle range and then rejoin the road after a railway crossing. From Maryburgh you follow Sustrans Route 1 south, leaving the cycle route at Monadh Mòr to take a beautiful gravel track through the forest followed by a singletrack into Tore. From here the route rejoins the Sustrans route, before another path through woodland takes you to Littleburn and past the Clootie Well at Munlochy. Clootie wells are linked to ancient healing traditions: a rag – or cloot – would be dipped in the well and tied to a tree in the hope that an ailment would fade as the rag disintegrated. If you are leaving an offering, please make sure it is small, appropriate and biodegradable: pure wool or pure cotton are best for the environment.

After Munlochy the route continues on a mixture of scenic roads and paths south towards Inverness. After passing the Kessock Bridge on Sustrans Route 1 you follow the cycling route into the Capital of the Highlands to finish at Inverness railway station. From here the From Coast to Barrel (page 141) and A Scottish Hostelling Adventure (page 151) routes offer onward journeys, as do the Caledonia Way and Badger Divide (page 148).

BIKE SHOPS AND HIRE
· Ticket to Ride, Inverness (hire).
  T: 01463 419 160
· Velocity Café & Bicycle Workshop, Inverness (shop) –
  www.velocitylove.co.uk
· Bikes of Inverness, Inverness (shop).
  T: 01463 225 965
· Highland Bikes, Inverness (shop).
  T: 01463 234 789
· Alpine Bikes @ Tiso, Inverness (shop).
  T: 01463 729 171
· Ullapool Bike Hire, Ullapool (hire).
  T: 07731 796 206
· LC24 Cycle Repair, Alness (service).
  T: 07725 740 813
· Dryburgh Cycles, Dingwall (shop).
  T: 01349 862 163

VIDEO INSPIRATION

L–R: *At the start of the Bealach na Bà; gravel track across Lochluichart wind farm.*

SPOTLIGHT MARK BEAUMONT

THE FASTEST MAN TO CYCLE THE NORTH COAST 500
@MrMarkBeaumont

Mark lives with his family in Edinburgh and is best known for his record double: in 2008 he set a world record of 194 days for circumnavigating the world by bicycle, a record which he bettered in 2017 in an astonishing 78 days, 14 hours and 40 minutes. On 25 September 2022, Mark set a new record for cycling the North Coast 500 with a time of 28 hours and 35 minutes, beating Robbie Mitchell's record. Mark had set the inaugural record in 2015, when the route was launched, with a time of 37 hours and 58 minutes.

'Your view is limited on the time trial bike of course. It's hard to explain to a non-cyclist, but you're still very aware of the world around you. I would argue that even though my view is a lot more down and limited than on a hybrid bike or on a touring bike, I'm still far more aware, in terms of all my senses, of the world around me than somebody who's cocooned in a car. Because you're connected to the climbs, you're aware of every twist and turn, any rise and fall of the road. You hear the sheep on the roadside, the wind and nature. So, you're very connected to the world around you, as only a cyclist would understand. For sure you've got a limited view of the road in front of you, and you can't see around you. But that idea that you missed the journey because you're not

THE ROUTE

At 516 miles (830 kilometres) long, the North Coast 500 (*www.northcoast500.com*) is one of the world's most beautiful road trips, with stunning coastal scenery, white sandy beaches, rugged mountains and remote fishing villages.

Mark's highlights of the route: *'I love it up in the North West. Slightly off the route by Achiltibuie and around the Summer Isles – there's just so much to explore. There's a huge area which is a Scottish Wildlife Trust reserve. And a little bit further up from that you've got these extraordinary beaches. So, that whole top-left corner. It's the hardest to get to, but it's incredibly rewarding in terms of its nature, its wildlife and its wild landscapes.'*

sitting up and looking around you: I still think if you include all your senses, you're much more connected to the true nature of the North Coast 500. Just how wild, how beautiful the changing road conditions are, the changing weather patterns, the coming of the night and then the coming of dawn; that whole journey in every sense of the world is very real. Because you are physically pushing yourself hard on a bicycle, I think that physical effort makes the appreciation of the landscape that you're going over all the greater. You're earning every mile, you're living it, as opposed to being a passenger in a car. So yes, if you define it as, "what was your scope of vision?" Yeah, that's pretty limited. But I've got very, very vivid memories of the character of that entire North Coast 500, because I was battling. I was absolutely battling on the bike.'

VIDEO INSPIRATION

L–R: *Sandwood Bay; coastal road from Applecross to Shieldaig; Mark approaching the Bealach na Bà; A832 between Dundonnell and Corrieshalloch; A862 near Kirkhill.*

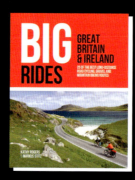

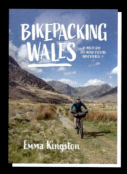